'Jo Owen has done it again. The challenges, old and new, facing leaders are laid out in easy to action chapters. You can either dive straight to a critical topic or read and learn across the breadth of leadership essentials.'

Michael Elliott, Vice President R&D, Gilead Sciences

'Turbo-charge your leadership skills the smart way! Packed full of intelligent insights, and implementable advice, *Smart Leadership* delivers everything required to elevate your trajectory as a successful leader.'

Professor Mike Caine, Associate Pro Vice-Chancellor, Loughborough University

'Jo Owen has done it again with a book on leadership that is fresh, thought-provoking and immediately useful. It is grounded in experience and the realities that leaders have to grapple with, and the author's experience shines through. Written engagingly and entertainingly, this book has something for people at all stages of their leadership journey.'

Tom Ravenscroft, Founder and CEO, the Skills Builder Partnership

'*Smart Leadership* is all the leadership books you'll need wrapped up into one. It is an enjoyable and insightful read, but will also be the book of reference that you will come back to over and over again as you face up to new leadership challenges.'

Graeme Duncan, CEO, Right to Succeed

SMART
LEADERSHIP

The Ultimate Handbook
for Great Leaders

JO OWEN

BLOOMSBURY BUSINESS
LONDON · OXFORD · NEW YORK · NEW DELHI · SYDNEY

BLOOMSBURY BUSINESS
Bloomsbury Publishing Plc
50 Bedford Square, London, WC1B 3DP, UK
29 Earlsfort Terrace, Dublin 2, Ireland

First published in Great Britain 2023

A catalogue record for this book is available from the British Library

Library of Congress Cataloging-in-Publication data has been applied for

ISBN: 978-1-3994-0378-8; eBook: 978-1-3994-0376-4

2 4 6 8 10 9 7 5 3 1

Typeset by Deanta Global Publishing Services, Chennai, India
Printed and bound in Great Britain by CPI Group (UK) Ltd, Croydon CR0 4YY

To find out more about our authors and books visit www.bloomsbury.com
and sign up for our newsletters

Contents

Introduction   1
About *Smart Leadership*   1
The leadership challenge   2
Leading in the twenty-first century   5

PART ONE: LEADING YOURSELF   7

1 Dare to dream, dare to act: the power of ambition   9

2 Stay positive: live longer, lead better   13

3 Be brave: the courage of leadership   17

4 Stay motivated: discover your inner drive   21

5 Build resilience: stay the course   25

6 Take responsibility: step up, not back   29

7 Reach out: no more lone heroes   34

8 Be (selectively) unreasonable: the dark side of leadership   37

9 Manage your energy: avoid burnout and stress   41

PART TWO: LEADING TASKS   45

10 Use time well   47

11 Meet with purpose   50

12 Talk to persuade   53

13 Present to persuade   60

14 Write with impact   64

15 Read (and listen) with purpose   66

16 Work the numbers   68

PART THREE: LEADING PEOPLE   **71**

17 Set goals   73

18 Coach for performance   77

19 Giving feedback   82

20 Dealing with poor performance   85

21 Dealing with difficult people   89

22 Lead your boss   92

23 Become the leader people want to follow   96

24 Become the trusted colleague   100

PART FOUR: LEADING TEAMS   **105**

25 Select the right team   107

26 Create a motivated team   110

27 Be a motivational team leader   117

28 Lead teams you cannot see   120

29 Build your remote or hybrid team   124

30 Delegate well   128

31 Know your role   132

PART FIVE: LEADING ORGANIZATIONS 135

32 Take control   137

33 Make change happen   141

34 Manage projects   147

35 Grow your influence across the organization   151

36 Fighting battles   155

37 Turn crises into opportunities   158

PART SIX: LEADING STRATEGY 163

38 How to have a strategic conversation   165

39 The language of strategy   170

40 Developing strategy in the middle of the organization   173

41 Developing strategy for the whole organization   176

PART SEVEN: MANAGE YOUR CAREER 181

42 Learn your unique success formula   183

43 Gain promotion   186

44 Manage your career   190

Index   195

Introduction

About *Smart Leadership*

Smart Leadership is about smart leaders at all levels; leadership is about what you do, not about your job title. As such you can lead at any level, whatever your formal job title may be. The book is intended to be your personal bookshelf coach to help you structure and accelerate your journey to successful leadership. It is about leadership as it is, not as it should be. It focuses on best practices, not on management theory.

Smart Leadership is for smart leaders and readers. It is, essentially, 44 books on leadership condensed into one; each of its 44 chapters deals with a classic leadership challenge. Each chapter offers a solution based on what works. The solution highlights one or two key insights for you to take away, and some core principles to work on. I assume that you are then smart enough to work out how to apply the insight and principles in ways which work for you in your context.

Although there is a logical sequence to the chapters in the book, you can read it in any order. The logic starts with leading yourself: leadership starts in your head, not in an office. It then progresses through leading tasks, teams, organizations and finally gets to dealing with strategy. You can read straight through, or you can dip in and out as you wish. Each chapter stands on its own, and you can use it independently of any other chapters. This means that, occasionally, I may have to repeat a point in two separate chapters, or make reference across chapters, although I have tried to keep this to a minimum. Because each chapter is short and succinct, they take careful reading: read less, but well.

Just as leadership is a team effort, so is writing a book. I am hugely grateful to Ian Hallsworth and the team at Bloomsbury for backing the idea and making it happen; and to my agent Jason Bartholomew for introducing me to Bloomsbury. I would also like to thank Allie Collins, senior editor, as well as my copy editor, Chris Stone, and the sales, marketing and publicity teams at Bloomsbury who ensured that *Smart Leadership* received the oxygen of publicity and trade support that any book needs. As ever, my wife Hiromi has been a rock of support, even when she became an involuntary book widow during the writing process.

Above all I would like to thank everyone who contributed their experience and insight to this book. I have worked with over 100 of the best, and a couple of the worst, organizations on this planet and I have learned from them all. The research for this book is based on many thousands of years of experience which contributors have given to me in interviews, surveys and observation.

A core theme of this book is that no leader is perfect, and the same is true of any book. Writers, like leaders, learn to take responsibility for any errors which may occur, despite all the help they get from their wonderful team. I apologize in advance for such errors and I hope they are trivial.

You can help improve this book, and so help other leaders, by suggesting corrections or improvements. You can reach me in my guise as either the author or as a keynote speaker at jo@ilead.guru, and you can find a regular leadership blog on my LinkedIn profile.

The leadership challenge

The challenge

Churchill described Russia as 'a riddle, wrapped in a mystery, inside an enigma'. He may as well have been talking about leadership. We all recognize a leader, but trying to define leadership is like trying to read smoke signals in the fog. It is an exercise in futility because every leader seems to be so different. The result is that the ideal leader looks like some implausible combination of Lord Nelson and Nelson Mandela, with bits of Mother Teresa and Genghis Khan thrown in for good measure.

The infinite variety of leadership role models generates an infinite number of leadership theories, all of which can be illustrated, but not proven, by reference to various leaders who conform to the theory. These theories are dangerous. They imply that you have to become like one of these leadership role models. But you will never succeed by trying to be someone else. Equally, you will not succeed just by being yourself and hoping that the world will recognize your innate genius and humanity.

Now we face two impossible problems:

- You cannot succeed by being someone else and you cannot succeed just by being yourself
- We don't know what we are aiming at because there is no good definition of a leader

It may now be very tempting to give up. But one of the few things all leaders have in common is that they do not give up in the face of adversity. So it is time to find solutions to these two problems:

You will never succeed by trying to be someone else

- Becoming a leader
- Defining leadership

The solution
Becoming a leader

The solution starts with an exercise. Try swapping Mother Teresa and Genghis Khan around. Imagine Mother Teresa leading the Mongol hordes on their rampage across Asia and to the edge of Europe. Now imagine Genghis Khan sorting out the slums of Calcutta. He probably would sort out the slums, but not to the advantage of the inhabitants. This contrast leads to four useful discoveries about how you can become a leader:

1. *Leadership is contextual.* What works in one context may not work in another context. The best leaders are not universal leaders: they succeed in one context. Churchill had his finest hour in wartime and was completely forgettable as a peacetime Prime Minister: same person, same role, but different contexts led to different results. As a leader, you have to find the context that works for you.
2. *No leader gets ticks in all the boxes.* There is no such thing as the perfect leader. There is only a leader who works in a context. This is wonderful news. You do not need to be perfect to succeed, but you need some signature strengths which sustain you. And you do not need to be perfect before you step up to a leadership role, because no leader is perfect. Be bold: have the courage to step up.
3. *Leadership is a team sport.* Because no leader gets ticks in all the boxes, they need people around them who fill in for their

weaknesses. No leader succeeds alone. Even Napoleon wanted generals, as long as they were lucky. As a leader, you have to build the right team to support you.

4. *You can lead on your terms.* There is a solution to the riddle about not succeeding as a leader by being someone else, or just by being yourself: you have to be the best of who you are. You have to find the context which plays to your strengths. *Smart Leadership* does not ask you to conform to an ideal: it shows you how you can be the best of who you are.

Defining leadership

Although we have some useful clues on how to become a leader, we still lack a viable definition of leadership. If we can't define leadership, then we don't know what we are aiming for. Similarly, if you don't know where the target is, you are unlikely to hit it. Most of the definitions of leadership do not stand up to challenge, but one definition has stood the test of time and proves to be very useful. Here it is:

Leaders take people where they would not have got by themselves.

At first that seems a little dull, but actually it is revolutionary for two reasons:

Leadership is about what you do, not about your title. There are plenty of people with grand titles such as CEO, President or even Prime Minister who fail this test: they are drifting with the tide rather than leading. But at the same time, there are many people lower in the organization who are leading. If you are a team leader who develops a new way of working for your team, then you are leading.

Change is at the heart of leadership. All managers know that maintaining the status quo is very hard, because the natural order of organizational life is for things to go wrong: experienced people leave, targets are raised, deadlines are brought forward, other departments compete for the same limited pot of budget and support, suppliers let you down and customers change their mind and always want more. But leaders have to do all this and more. Leaders take people where they would not have got by themselves: that means they don't just make incremental improvements, they imagine and implement whole new ways of doing things.

Leading in the twenty-first century

The challenge

Leadership is becoming harder, not easier.

In the nineteenth century, leadership was relatively simple. The bosses had the brains and the workers had the hands, with 'thinking' and 'doing' being seen as separate activities; the bosses had to be smart to lead largely uneducated masses. As a result, IQ was at the heart of leadership.

Leadership became harder in the twentieth century because the workers did something revolutionary: they became educated. This meant that they could do more, but at the same time they expected more. They could no longer be treated as unreliable units of production and, occasionally, consumption. Instead, they had to be treated like ... human beings. It was no longer enough for a leader to be a brain on sticks. Leaders had to learn the arts of dealing with people, or in other words, EQ (Emotional Quotient).

In the twenty-first century, things have become even harder. In the past, leaders made things happen through the people they controlled. Now, you have to make things happen through people you do not control, or who do not want to be controlled. You can only succeed with the support of other departments, with support of your bosses, and perhaps of suppliers and customers as well. Even the professionals on your team probably do not want to be managed: they want autonomy, not management. This calls for a whole new skills set around influence, persuasion, building networks of allies and support, and pushing your agenda and priorities. We can call these skills PQ, or Political Quotient: the art of making the organization you work for, work for you.

The great pandemic accentuated the twenty-first challenge of control. You now have to make things happen through people you may not control and may not even see all day. We have discovered that the office was a paradise for control freak managers who could interfere (or possibly help) at will by walking across the room. It is hard to micromanage people when you do not even know what they are wearing beneath the waistline. Hybrid working and WFH (working from home) has forced leaders to raise their game, because everything is harder when you cannot see and talk to your team all the time: even the basics of communicating, goal setting and delegating become harder. This is good news: if you can lead a remote team, you can lead any team.

Technology enabled the shift to hybrid working, but has made leadership even harder for leaders. Technology enables a consumer utopia where anything is available anywhere at any time. But on the other side of that bargain is a dystopian world where leaders have to be available to do anything, anywhere at any time. The technological shackles of email, internet, instant messaging and smart phones means that you can be on

If you can lead a remote team, you can lead any team

call 24/7 52 weeks a year. This is reflected in the data: in the past, it was the low paid who worked the most hours, now it is the highest paid and highest qualified who work the most hours. There may be justice in that, but the price of justice is stress and burnout at record levels. You have to learn to tame the technology beast. Technology should be the servant, not the master.

Twenty-first-century leaders need a rare combination of IQ, EQ and PQ: this book gives you the essence of all these skills.

The solution

These changes are good news for everyone.

Leaders are being forced to raise their game. That is good for followers who have had to endure mediocre management for too long. You have probably suffered your share of weak management, and it is not an enjoyable experience. Good leadership is good for followers: they perform better, they enjoy it more when they have the right role model to learn from.

The higher performance bar is good for (some) leaders as well. Mediocre managers will find themselves increasingly exposed. Even if their bosses do not find them out, their followers will. The most common reason for leaving a firm is to escape a toxic boss. A leader who can neither recruit nor retain the best talent will struggle to survive, let alone succeed. Raising the bar ensures that only the best leaders rise to the top.

Smart Leadership is intended to give you at least part of the solution to leadership in the twenty-first century. However, you cannot read a book and finish on page 208 as the complete leader. In practice, we all learn mainly from our own experience and observing the experience of colleagues and others. But this book can help you by making sense of the nonsense you encounter, by giving you structure to the random walk of experience, and by giving you practical tools to help you navigate your path to leadership.

Smart Leadership is your private coach, helping you to become the best of who you are. It will help you accelerate your leadership journey.

PART ONE

LEADING YOURSELF

1

Dare to dream, dare to act: the power of ambition

The challenge

Leaders are different from managers. Managers have a hard job sustaining and improving a legacy they have inherited from the previous manager. Leaders do not just sustain a legacy; they create a whole new legacy, taking people where they would not have got by themselves. Instead of working with today's reality, they challenge today's reality. They want to create the future, not sustain the past.

Organizations need great managers to run things, and a few great leaders to change things. If everyone is leading, you would have the chaos of constant revolution. If you have no leaders, the firm will slowly decay and be consigned to the dustbin of history. Leaders need managers and managers need leaders: they have to be able to work with and understand each other.

Leadership is not just a skill set, it is a mindset. Inevitably, a skilled leader will do better than an unskilled leader if all other things are equal. But all things very rarely are equal. Mindset often turns out to be the difference between a great manager and a great leader. Both may be equally skilled, but only the leader is ready to step up at moments of crisis, take risks and to challenge the way things are today.

Management mindset	Leadership mindset
Sustain a legacy	Create a new legacy
Maintain and improve	Disrupt and change
Focus on excellence	Find new ways of competing and working
Meet targets	Achieve the mission
Deal with today's reality	Create the future
Be reasonable	Be (selectively) unreasonable
Crisis as risk	Crisis as opportunity

We all have dreams of what we might do or could be. But most of those dreams die on first contact with reality: the dream takes too much risk, time and effort and in the meantime there is the rent to pay and the dog to feed. So it is not enough to dream; you have to dare to act as well.

Leadership is not just a skill set, it is a mindset

It might seem that you have to be born with the mindset of leadership: either you have the required ambition and courage, or you do not. This is not true. This book will show you how you can learn the mindset of leadership. Mindset is simply shorthand for habits of mind which we all have: normally our habits help us, but sometimes they can hold us back. As with all habits, we can choose to learn new habits if we want to. This book will show you how even courage is a habit which you can learn; it will then go on to show you how you can learn the skills of leadership as well.

But that leaves us with our first challenge: can you develop the sort of ambition that lets you not just dare to dream, but also dare to act?

The solution

The solution to the problem of ambition starts with ... a problem. If you want to lead, to take people where they would not have got by themselves, find a problem you face. And then solve it. The bigger the problem, the better. If you solve the problem of missing paper clips in the office, you are not really leading. If you find a big problem, you are forced to find a big solution. As soon as you start working on the big solution, you will find yourself thinking and acting like a leader. You will be finding ways to create a new future, to disrupt and change, to create a new legacy. You will be completely focused on your new mission. You will discover the importance of being selectively unreasonable: every time you hear 'no' you will simply regard that as a prelude to 'yes'. When you believe in your mission, you become a hard force to stop. You never accept excuses and you never accept 'no'.

Everyone can become a leader if they find a big enough problem and decide to tackle it. Even I have found myself being an accidental leader at least three times when I stumbled into three problems that I wanted to solve:

Never accept excuses and never accept 'no'

- Small and middle market firms are being ripped off by banks: high charges, poor service, no innovation. Solution: raise £1 billion to start a new middle market bank, which later became HBOS business banking.
- Schools in deprived areas can't recruit great graduates to be teachers. Solution: start Teach First, which became the UK's largest graduate recruiter.
- Education in low-income countries suffers because teachers are disengaged and often poorly treated. Solution: start a global NGO (STIR Education) to help millions of officials, teachers and children rediscover their intrinsic motivation for education.

I knew nothing about banking or education when I started to attack these challenges. As a leader, you do not need to be the expert. There are many experts who know the answer. But they are experts, not leaders. Experts do the thinking, leaders bring the experts together and make it happen. So how do you dare to act on your dream?

You do not learn the art of cliff diving by jumping off the first cliff you see. You learn in small steps, starting by learning to swim and then diving into a pool from its side. You can take on the biggest challenge with the smallest step: talk to someone about the problem and your idea. That costs you nothing and risks nothing. Then talk to more people. Talk to experts. Talk to backers. When some people reject you, find others who will support you. Slowly, you will refine your idea and build your coalition of support. Suddenly, you will find yourself doing something you never imagined possible. You will have become a leader, even if you never intended to be a leader.

Dare to dream and dare to act

The bigger the idea, the better. Big ideas get far more engagement than small ideas. It was easier for me to ask for £1 billion investment than it was to ask for a £1,000 overdraft, even though it was the same bank I had been talking to at different times. For £1 billion, you talk to the CEO who can make decisions. For £1,000 you talk to a disempowered staffer who is constrained by processes, procedures and protocols.

You can dare to dream and dare to act. You can learn the ambition which all leaders need. Find a big problem and solve it. Start with small and risk free steps: talk to people to improve your solution and build your coalition.

Think big, start small and scale fast.

2

Stay positive: live longer, lead better

The challenge

Optimists live longer and perform better than pessimists. Optimism comes from within. No one can tell you to be optimistic or positive. If you are not positive, no one else can be positive for you. Who wants to work for a gloomy and pessimistic leader? Pessimistic leaders find they have pessimistic teams, which is a recipe for failure.

Here are five questions which will show how optimistic or pessimistic you are:

- Do you trust other people?
- Do good things happen to you?
- Is the world becoming a better place?
- Do you expect to live better than your parents?
- Do you enjoy your current role?

If you answered 'yes' easily to all of the questions above, you are a natural optimist and you do not need to read the rest of this section. Natural pessimists will answer 'no'. Pessimism is not just a personal challenge: it is a leadership challenge. Followers want hope, certainty and clarity. They do not want gloom and ambiguity. Pessimists have to learn to wear the mask

Optimists live longer and perform better than pessimists

of leadership so that they become the leader people want to follow. This section shows how.

Most people find that they are in the middle. On a good day we can be optimistic and positive. On a bad day, we may struggle. Leaders are not judged by how they behave when they are in easy street. They are judged by how they behave when things are tough. It pays to learn to be positive in tough times, not just in good times.

The solution

Being optimistic and pessimistic is about how we react to the world. We cannot control the world, but we can control how we react to it. We can choose how we react: that means we can choose to have a positive or negative outlook on life. Four exercises will help you see the world differently and lead differently.

Exercise one: how's your day?

A simple test will make the point. First, note down all the things that went wrong today: missed traffic lights, annoying emails, not finding a good parking space and so on. Do not do this exercise for too long: it is a good way to start feeling bad. Instead, do the alternative exercise: note all the good things which happened today, from the moment you woke up. When I do this exercise with groups, I am overwhelmed by the number of great things which people discover within moments of waking up: waking up in a warm house on a cold day; light at the flick of a switch; clean hot and cold running water at the turn of a tap; seeing the family and so on.

If you are having a bad day, take a moment to remember all the mundane miracles of modern life and the friends and family around you. It will help you regain some perspective.

Exercise two: hunt the good stuff

This formalizes exercise one, and is a proven way to help change the way you see the world. At the end of each day, write down three good things about the day. Writing is important: it focuses your mind and makes the exercise deliberate and memorable. Do this for 30 days. By the end of the month, you will find that you routinely start noticing all the good things in life. You start hunting the good stuff, not the bad stuff, in life. That is a sea change in perspective.

As a variation on this exercise you might try noting down three things you learned, or three ways in which you helped others or were helped. Each time, the goal is to start being more aware of what is good in life, not just what is bad or threatening.

> **Start hunting the good stuff, not the bad stuff, in life**

Exercise three: the prince and princess

Here is an offer I make to many groups. I can let you travel in my time machine and you can live (with your friends and family, if you want) as a prince or princess 250 years ago. Would you like to take up this offer?

At first sight, this seems to be an irresistible offer. You will be swapping hot and cold running water for hot and cold running servants. But you will also be living without indoor sanitation, dentistry, pain killers, central heating or air conditioning, electricity, internet, TV, telephones, social media, cars, planes etc. Over 90 per cent of people choose to live today, with all its challenges, rather than live as a prince or princess in the past.

Once you discover that your life is better than that of a prince or princess in the past, it becomes easier to appreciate how lucky we are today.

Exercise four: positive leadership

Your followers will judge you by how you behave when the going gets tough. These are the memorable moments of truth when reputations are built or destroyed. Instinctive reactions in a crisis are helpful if you need to jump out of the way of an oncoming car, but the fight or flight reaction is unhelpful at work: you do not want to fight colleagues and you do not want to run away from the challenge.

> **You always have a choice about how you behave**

Remember that you always have a choice about how you feel and how you behave. Ideally, you will feel and act like the positive leader in the table below. But even if you are feeling like the negative leader, you can still choose to wear the mask of leadership and behave like the positive leader.

Negative leadership	Positive leadership
Analyse what went wrong	Drive to action
Look to the past	Focus on the future
Blame colleagues	Seek colleagues' support
Focus on problems	Find solutions
See risks and threats	See opportunities
Tension and aggression	Calmness and hope

Just as feelings can dictate behaviour, so behaviour can dictate feelings. By forcing yourself to behave positively, you will start to feel positive as well. You can create a virtuous circle of positivity for yourself.

3

Be brave: the courage of leadership

The challenge

In the past leaders needed courage to face down enemies and lead their troops into battle. So what has that got to do with leading in an office or virtual world? Leaders today still need courage, of a different sort. As a leader you need courage to:

- Take people where they would not have got by themselves
- Challenge and change the status quo
- Have difficult conversations with colleagues
- Make difficult and unpopular decisions
- Step up, not back, at moments of crisis and ambiguity
- Risk failure by trying new things and starting new projects
- Learn new skills and go outside your comfort zone of success
- Seek the accountability and responsibility that comes with leadership

The problem is that there is no course that teaches you courage. Fortunately, courage does not have to be in your genes, otherwise a simple genetic test at the start of your career would determine whether you are allowed to move on to the leadership track or not. Although there is no courage course on an MBA or elsewhere, courage is something you can learn. This chapter shows you how you can acquire the courage of a leader.

Step up, not back, at moments of crisis

The solution

Mountaineers go where others fear to tread. Climbing looks, and can be, crazy dangerous. Firefighters are prepared to go into burning buildings to rescue people. Insanely dangerous. The Royal Marine Commandos are often the first into the most hostile, ambiguous and dangerous situations: that appears to be utterly mad. So how do such different groups land up being able to do such courageous things? In my work with each of these groups, there is a consistent answer which applies just as well to leading in an office. The three keys to learning courage are:

1. Training in incremental steps
2. Structure and support
3. Practise, practise, practise

1. Training in incremental steps

The training for firefighters, Royal Marines and mountaineers all starts the same way: simply. Start with simple tasks, for instance:

- *Firefighters.* Start by learning how to put on basic kit, put out a fire in a frying pan and how to handle a small ladder. Slowly, introduce more sophisticated kit, larger fires and longer ladders. Eventually, dealing with large burning buildings is routine and they know what to do.
- *Mountaineers.* A child wanted to climb Everest. His starting point was to spend (part of) a night under canvas in the garden. Get used to the routines of camping and then learn to walk safely in the hills. Safely introduce climbing techniques on an indoor wall with harnesses. Then introduce more challenging climbs and more adverse camping conditions. Everest beckons.
- *Royal Marine Commandos.* The pre-joining fitness programme for the Commandos starts with running a mile in eight minutes. Even grandpa could do that, on a good day. Slowly, the physical demands ramp up and the required skills are trained. After 16 months of intense training, successful candidates become officers.

This training shows that courage is context specific. Firefighters would not feel comfortable climbing Everest, and mountaineers would not feel comfortable going into a hostile firefight. As one mountaineer said: 'Show me a cliff and I will climb it. Ask me to sell double glazing and I will run a mile.' Learn the skills of leadership and you will appear to have the courage of a leader: a brave leader is a skilled leader doing what they know best.

2. Structure and support

Training for Royal Marines, firefighters and mountaineers is highly structured and closely supervised, unlike leadership learning. Most leadership journeys are a random walk of experience. There is minimal structure and not much active support for your learning. This makes learning to lead highly inefficient. As a leader you have to put as much structure and support into your learning journey as you can. That means:

- Make sure you get the right assignments, bosses and experiences at the right time. Don't let others control your career for you.
- Get help and frequent feedback from your boss, so that there are no surprises at the year-end review. If your boss is unwilling or unable to be your coach, find someone (even pay for someone) to be your coach. A good coach will help you see a different perspective, learn fast and structure your thoughts.
- Learn from your experience and your colleagues in a structured way: see chapter 42. Debrief after key events and important meetings so that you learn from them.

3. Practise, practise, practise

Ten thousand hours is frequently quoted as the amount of time you need to truly master any skill. We can debate how long mastery of courage takes, but it is clear you need to keep practising. For instance, public speaking takes courage. The first two steps of learning courage apply: start with small and simple talks to friends or close colleagues and then get structured feedback and support. But ultimately, you need to practise, practise and practise. This is just what the firefighters, mountaineers and Royal Marines do. Training does not stop after the initial training. Training never stops, so that you can reinforce and build on your basic skills.

Most leadership journeys are a random walk of experience

You need courage to deal with unfamiliar situations where you lack the experience or skills to succeed. The more you practise, the more the unfamiliar becomes familiar. Practise and mastery turns a risky event into a routine event. What looks brave to others will be second nature to you. You will have learned courage.

4

Stay motivated: discover your inner drive

The challenge

You cannot have high performance and low motivation. And yet there is a quiet epidemic of low motivation at work. Different surveys estimate that as few as 15–30 per cent of employees feel motivated at work.

As a leader, you need to be motivated to put in the extra discretionary effort; to take on the new initiative; to turn a good enough project into a great project; to sustain yourself when adversity strikes. And if you are not motivated, your team will not be motivated. You have to be a role model for them. But you cannot tell anyone to be motivated, or positive or happy. Motivation comes from within.

The challenge is to stay motivated for the 30–40 year marathon of your leadership career. As a professional you are probably already intrinsically motivated to perform well, because professionals have pride in who they are and how they perform. So the challenge is not to discover the secret of motivation. The challenge is to create the conditions in which you and your intrinsic motivation will flourish.

You cannot have high performance and low motivation

Understanding how you can create the conditions where you are motivated is the mirror image of how you can create the conditions for your team to be motivated (chapter 26): the principles are exactly the same. They are sufficiently important to be worth repeating.

The solution

Work with millions of officials, teachers and children around the world shows that you can sustain your intrinsic motivation where four conditions are in place. These four conditions are the RAMP model, which stands for:

- Relationships that are positive. You are likely to perform best when you have a supportive boss and supportive colleagues, friends and family. Toxic bosses are the #1 reason why people quit their jobs: people do not quit their firm, they quit their boss.
- Autonomy, because professionals do not need or want to be micromanaged. You flourish when you are trusted to perform, not controlled to perform.
- Mastery, because it is hard to be motivated when you lack the skills for today's role and you are not growing the skills you need for the role you want tomorrow.
- Purpose: if you have a clear goal and meaning in your work, you are more likely to keep going through adversity and make the extra effort all leaders need to make.

The RAMP model is an easy way to rate your current situation and see where you might want to improve. Relationships, autonomy and mastery are largely self-explanatory. Perhaps the most important and most challenging part of the RAMP model is purpose, which we will explore more here.

Purpose

This comes from three sources:

1. Extrinsic rewards
2. Organizational purpose
3. Job crafting

1. *Extrinsic rewards*, such as pay and conditions motivate and demotivate. The carrot of a big bonus can focus the mind and motivate you to work hard. It can also demotivate you, for two reasons.

First, if you get a big bonus but your colleague gets a bigger one then motivation turns to demotivation. Bonuses are not just about money: they are about recognition and status. Being told that you are lower status, worth less and recognized less than your colleagues is never going to be motivational.

Second, extrinsic rewards put you on the hedonic treadmill. Essentially, there is no point at which enough is enough. We are all needs junkies and we all want more. At first you may have been happy to be given a bicycle; then you want a motorbike; then you want a car, followed by increasingly fancy cars until you graduate to a light aircraft, then a private jet and eventually you want to be the first billionaire to go to Mars. Once you are used to the jet lifestyle, going back to the bicycle lifestyle is unthinkable. The hedonic treadmill has no reverse gear: it keeps pushing to make us want more and more and to keep up with our peers who always seem to have something we don't have.

The hedonic treadmill has no reverse gear

If you step on to the hedonic treadmill, be aware that it is very hard to get off unless you are pushed off. The motivation to get richer has no end point.

2. Organizational purpose

History is littered with the corpses of people who have made huge sacrifices to die for their country, their religion or their beliefs. Today, you will find many highly motivated and highly talented people working for poor pay and conditions in the armed forces, for charities and for religious groups. Being part of something bigger than yourself, which has real meaning and purpose in itself, is highly motivating if you share the belief of the organization.

Even if you find your calling in a mission-driven organization, you will still need the other three pillars of motivation: positive relationships, autonomy and mastery. Some of the best purpose-driven organizations, such as the elite elements of the armed forces, deliberately work on these three pillars. Other purpose-driven organizations regard purpose as a substitute for good management. Choose carefully.

3. Job crafting: discovering personal purpose in your work

Most work exists in a grey zone of motivation, which is reflected in low levels of motivation at work. The extrinsic rewards may be fair but modest, and there is no uplifting sense of moral purpose in the firm. It is hard to get excited about helping anonymous shareholders get marginally richer.

In this grey space, you have to discover why work has meaning and purpose to you. All work provides some combination of: status and identity; a social structure with colleagues; structure and meaning to each day. These give work some meaning and provide a platform for motivation. It is easy to dismiss the importance of these, until you are out of a job. Then you discover that they are very important indeed.

Ideally, you will find more purpose in your work. There are two classic routes to discovering job purpose: mastery (again) and helping others.

Mastery is in itself highly motivational. To see a potter, musician or other crafts person totally absorbed in their work, even after 50 years, is to witness the power of mastery to motivate. Attempting to become the best in your field, to be a role model for others and to be recognized as a leading expert gives you a personal mission which will last a lifetime.

Helping others is what mission-driven organizations claim to do and it sustains the motivation of people who work there. In practice, what you do helps other people in some way. Customers would not pay for your products or services if you were not helping them. Take pride in how you make a positive difference to the world and to others. Even if you have a support role far from the customer, customers still need you to help deliver what they need, and your colleagues need your help and support to perform as well. You can work for yourself (extrinsic rewards of pay and promotion) and you can discover the intrinsic reward of helping others at the same time. Job crafting helps you double your sources of motivation.

Your motivation is your responsibility

Never wait to be motivated, because you will have a very long wait. As a leader, you have to take responsibility and that includes taking responsibility for how you feel, how you act and how you behave. Your motivation is your responsibility: create or find the conditions where your intrinsic motivation can flourish.

5

Build resilience: stay the course

The challenge

To succeed, first you must survive. As a leader, you have to take risks and push boundaries. If you have never failed, you have never tried hard enough. When you have a major setback, you can find yourself in a very dark and lonely place. At such moments, the difference between success and failure is as simple as not giving up.

You should never prepare to fail, but you can prepare to respond to setbacks so that first you survive, and then you can succeed. This section shows how you can prepare for adversity, and it comes with a warning. Resilience has become a fashionable topic and some firms now give resilience training. That can be helpful, but is too often an excuse for bad management practices where long hours and stress are commonplace. You should not have to train staff to be **Adversity should be a bug, not a feature, of corporate life** resilient in the face of bad management: you should ensure that there is good management. Resilience helps you deal with adversity which should be a bug, not a feature, of corporate life.

The solution

Resilience in adversity is about how you are and how you react in the moment.

How you are

How you are is the mindset you choose to cultivate, which is covered in this part of the book. To make the point clear, you will be more resilient if you are:

- *Ambitious.* When you are highly driven to achieve a goal, you may hit a stumbling block and fall but you will pick yourself up again to chase your dream. If you have nothing to fight for, you will have no incentive to fight back against the slings and arrows of outrageous fortune.
- *Positive.* The positive mindset encourages resilience in adversity because it will help you focus on solutions, not problems; you will drive to action instead of analysing adversity; you will see opportunity where others can only see problems.
- *Reaching out.* Adversity can be lonely and is exactly the time we need practical and moral support. By building relationships in good times, you have the support you need in hard times.
- *Managing your energy.* Adversity can lead to apathy or to over-exertion: neither are helpful responses. Knowing how to sustain peak performance is essential at moments of truth when the world seems to be conspiring against you. Stay goal focused; take small steps; stay fresh by taking breaks and creating boundaries between work and home.

How you react

Resilience is about how you mentally react to adversity. Unfortunately, we can be our own worst critics when it comes to our internal chatter. We say things to ourselves that we would never say to others. In good times, this critical chatter helps us stay alert to danger. In hard times, it becomes toxic and demoralizing. It is easy to start ruminating on misfortune and then catastrophizing.

Manage your internal chatter so that it helps you, not hinders you. Here are three ways you can manage your internal chatter better:

Be aware of your internal chatter and to be ready to challenge it.

If you find yourself beating yourself up, challenge your chatter. Instead of letting it be your own worst critic, ask it to act as your best friend. What would your best friend be telling you at moments like this? The chances are that it will be more comforting, positive and productive than ruminating on misfortune. Invite your best friend into your chatter.

Watch the movie, not the snapshot.

In adversity it is easy to see the picture which looks like a disaster zone. It then becomes easy to give up. Instead of looking at the picture, watch the movie. Look back on what you have achieved, what you have learned and how much you have progressed over the last few years. That will give you the evidence you need to show that you can succeed, and you can start to plan the rest of the movie where the hero overcomes the crisis to achieve success. Visualizing past success gives you confidence; visualizing future success gives you focus on what you can and should do next.

Stop catastrophizing.

When things go wrong, it is easy to start believing that the sky will fall down. You know you are catastrophizing when your internal chatter starts using absolute words such as 'Never, always, no one, nothing, everyone'. For instance: 'nothing is working, no one is supporting me and everything I try always goes wrong'. As soon as you start thinking that, your mind will find plenty of evidence to support your narrative. You will find evidence of where things went wrong and people did not support you. The narrative quickly becomes the truth and then you are doomed: you may as well give up there and then.

Adversity is an opportunity

The first step to dealing with catastrophic thinking is to recognize that you are catastrophizing. The use of absolute words ('no one, always, nothing' etc.) should raise a big red flag for you. Instead of finding evidence to confirm your belief, challenge yourself to find evidence which points in the opposite direction. Perhaps there is one person who supports you sometimes, perhaps there are one or two things you do which work.

Learn and grow. Adversity is an opportunity to learn and grow, although it is the sort of opportunity you probably do not want to welcome into your life every day of the week. We learn our most valuable lessons fastest when we face hard times. They are lessons you can only gain from first-hand experience: managing yourself, coping with difficult times and people, sustaining energy and motivation.

Adversity is when you also grow: as Nietzsche nearly said 'that which does not break you makes you stronger'. Dealing with adversity enables you to deal with adversity more easily next time: once you have lived through the movie a few times, you know the plot and you know what to expect and how to react. See adversity as a positive challenge for you to learn and grow. Visualize your positive outcome where you come out stronger and better than before, and then work to that goal. Turn adversity to advantage.

6

Take responsibility: step up, not back

The challenge

The responsibility challenge comes in two flavours:

- Embracing accountability when it is given
- Stepping up to take on more responsibility

Embracing accountability when it is given

The good news is that we live in an era of high autonomy. Most professionals crave autonomy, and want even more of it.

The bad news is that autonomy is not a free lunch. Autonomy and accountability march hand in hand. More autonomy leads to more accountability. Your success or failure becomes more transparent. Professionals enjoy being held to account for success more than they enjoy being held to account for setbacks. This can make them reluctant to take on the most challenging and stretching tasks. The most challenging tasks are where you will learn and grow the most and you will stake your claim to fame. You have to find ways to embrace accountability as your ally, not your foe.

Autonomy and accountability march hand in hand

Stepping up to take on more responsibility

As a leader, you have to embrace responsibility and accountability. The buck stops here: with you. But many potential leaders hesitate to step up, leaving the way open to less talented but more ambitious and confident rivals. If you wait to be asked to lead, you will have a very long wait.

Leaders do not wait to be asked
Take every opportunity to lead, to learn and to prove yourself. Leaders learn to step up, not step back.

The solution

Embracing accountability when it is given

Accountability is wonderful, provided you succeed. Your goal is not to take on mission impossible and to fail heroically. Accepting a 'challenging' project is very macho, and is a recipe for sleepless nights and stress. Assignments are like battles: they are won or lost before they start. Your goal is to make sure that you are set up for success every time you take on a new responsibility. If you can do this, you will find that you can embrace accountability, not shy away from it.

The easiest way to set yourself up for success is to have the success conversation with whoever is asking you to take on this new assignment, project or accountability. The success conversation has a simple focus: 'how can we set this up for success?' Most managers like this conversation: it shows that you are serious about the assignment. They need you to succeed because they want to look good as well. It is a good discussion for you and your boss.

Ask every question you need to make sure you are set up to succeed. Here are the classic questions to ask:

- *Goal clarity*: what is the goal? What does a great outcome look like and what does an acceptable outcome look like? What is the problem we are solving and who are we solving it for? Why are we focused on this goal now as opposed to all the other priorities in the business?
- *Resources:* What is the budget? Who else will be on the team? Is this important enough to merit the A team or is it a low priority which only needs the B team? Where does this sit with my other priorities? Can I shift some of my lesser responsibilities on to other people?
- *Obstacles:* what are the major obstacles and risks we face, and what can we do to mitigate them? Who is sponsoring this and do they

have enough power to deal with all the political obstacles we will face and to gain the support and resources we need?

- *Timing:* what is the deadline and what are the major check points? Who will monitor progress and how often will we report on progress?

If the project is genuinely worthwhile, you will discover good answers to these questions. If you find that you are going to be given the B team, you will have no powerful sponsor, and that the time and resources do not match the goal, you can reasonably challenge the assignment. There is no point in being set up to fail. It is better to have a difficult conversation about expectations at the start, than to have an impossible conversation about results at the end.

Learn to lean into accountability by setting yourself up for success.

Stepping up to take on more responsibility

A surprising number of leaders suffer imposter syndrome: they do not really believe that they belong in a top leadership role. If you don't step up, others will happily take your place. Imposter syndrome has its source in two stories we tell ourselves:

- I'm not good enough
- I don't belong

'I'm not good enough' is probably true for every leader, because no leader gets ticks in all the boxes. This is the essential truth to focus on. No one is ever 100 per cent ready for the next big role. You always have to learn on the job. If you try to be 100 per cent ready, you will never get there. Do not focus on your weaknesses. Focus on your strengths: do you have enough strengths which are relevant to the job? Those strengths are your platform for success. And there is an antidote to the problem that no leader gets ticks in all the boxes: leadership is a team sport. No matter how good you are, you need to build a team around you. Hire people who balance your weaknesses with their strengths.

If you go for a job and are rejected, the 'I'm not good enough' script can be given a vicious twist by the selection panel. They will feel compelled to make up a story about why you were not good enough. The danger is that you believe their story and then lose a couple of years working on the weaknesses that the selection panel claimed to have found. There are several problems with this:

- The selection panel may well be wrong
- You will not succeed by working on your weaknesses
- You probably were good enough, but there was another candidate who either was better, or was a better fit, or interviewed better or got lucky

Accept that no leader gets ticks in all the boxes. You will learn in role and you are good enough to step up when you have strengths to support you. Never give up trying to find the leadership role you want, don't let others steal what should be yours.

'*I don't belong*' is particularly hard for people who do not come from traditional leadership backgrounds. If you are male, white and affluent you see plenty of leadership role models who look and act like yourself. You learn how to dress and act without thinking about it. You probably do not have to waste time worrying about whether and when to wear high heels. If

The consequences of perceptions are real

you come from a more marginalized group you may find you are being asked to make tea or take minutes. Showing you belong is an extra hurdle that is placed in front of you.

The first step to dealing with the belonging challenge is to recognize that it is a story which says more about society than it does about you. If you are good enough to lead, then you belong: period. But you still have to deal with the perceptions of others: perceptions may be false, the consequences of perceptions are real. You have three choices, none of which are ideal:

- Act the part, and enjoy the performance. Follow the unwritten rules of leadership where you work, and use them to your advantage. As a relative outsider, you probably observe and understand the rules better than insiders who have never had to think about them. This means you can take great pleasure in occasionally and deliberately flouting the established etiquette.
- Play to your own rules. Do not pretend to be something you are not. Double down on performing as an outstanding leader and let

others adapt to you instead of you adapting to them: high risk, high reward.
- Move to a context which aligns more with who you are and how you are. Some firms and industries are much more diverse than others. Go where you are most likely to succeed.

We all tell ourselves stories about who we are and how we are. Most of the time, those stories help us navigate life well. Occasionally, those stories are unhelpful and need to be challenged. Impostor syndrome is an unhelpful story which you must challenge if you are to lead.

7

Reach out: no more lone heroes

The challenge

The movies and history teach us exactly the wrong lessons about leadership. In the movies the lone hero saves the world and defeats evil. History is also replete with heroes and villains who appear to lead countries to triumph or disaster. The hero view of leadership is alive and well in airport bookshops which are replete with self-serving, ghost written, autobiographies of billionaires and high-profile leaders.

Movies, history and autobiographies are dangerous because they imply you succeed or fail by yourself, and that you have to do it all yourself. The reality is that lone heroes, and lone villains, never succeed by themselves: they need an army of supporters.

Your leadership journey starts with the transition from being a worker or staffer to being a first line manager. At that moment, your mindset has to change from asking 'how do I do this?' to 'who can do this?' If you try to do it all, you will not have enough hours in the day and you will stress out, burn out and drop out. If you reach out to others you will discover the alchemy of leadership: you can deliver far more than eight hours of productive work per day. You can deliver thousands of hours of productive work per day, if you have a large enough team.

A problem shared is a problem halved, and a joy shared is a joy doubled

The 'reach out' challenge is not just professional: it is personal as well. You cannot bear the burdens of the world alone. Having supportive friends and family outside work creates perspective and eases the burden. A problem shared is a problem halved, and a joy shared is a joy doubled.

The solution

Reaching out and building support sounds obvious, but presents two stumbling blocks, which are the opposite of each other:

- Why would you want to become dependent on other people?
- Why would anyone want to support you, anyway?

Why would you want to become dependent on other people?
This is the delegation problem, covered in chapter 30. The core challenge is that managers are nervous about letting go. As soon as you delegate, your success becomes dependent on someone else. A better way to look at it is that as soon as you delegate, you enhance your chances of success:

- You have more time to invest in your own priorities
- A good team may come up with better solutions than you alone could have imagined

If you find it hard to delegate to your team, that shows that you do not trust your team. That lack of trust is toxic to your team who will become increasingly demotivated and low performing, which will reinforce your lack of trust and create a vicious circle which leads to disaster. There are two antidotes to this:

- Learn to delegate well, which reduces the perceived risk of delegation
- Recruit the right team

If you find it hard to delegate, then either you have the wrong team or your team has the wrong boss.

Why would anyone want to support you, anyway?
A consistent theme of this book is that in today's world you have to become the leader people want to follow, not the leader they have to follow. The days of coercive leadership, when people did as they were told, are long over.

> **When you accept excuses, you accept failure**

The key insight is that you do not need to be popular: you need to be trusted and respected. Popularity leads to weakness because it means you always compromise: you accept excuses about why deadlines should be extended and goals reduced. When you accept excuses, you accept failure.

The keys to becoming trusted and respected are:

- *Build personal trust* (chapter 24). This is about always doing as you say. The real trap is rarely in the doing, it is in the saying: be crystal clear about expectations because colleagues often hear what they want to hear, not what they need to hear.
- *Listening* (chapter 15). In a time starved world, listening is flattering: it implies you care for, and value, the other person's perspectives and insight. It is also a very good way of understanding their motivation, so that you can influence and persuade them better.
- *Show gratitude*, which is flattery on steroids. Who thinks that they are over-promoted, overpaid and over-recognized? Sadly, most people think the opposite. So when you recognize a colleague's genius, insight and excellence they are likely to think highly of your very fine judgement.
- *Be influential* (chapter 35) because colleagues are always attracted to power and success. You need a claim to fame in terms of expertise or achievement, and you need to be close to the agenda of the CEO which always has the highest priority in the firm.

8

Be (selectively) unreasonable: the dark side of leadership

The challenge

The world is not changed by reasonable people. We all remember Alexander the Great who conquered the entire known civilized world by the age of 30. Who remembers his cousin Alexander the Reasonable? Legendary co-founder of Apple, Steve Jobs, was said to have a reality distortion field. He distorted reality to fit his needs: reasonable people do not think like that and do not start Apple. As a result, even his colleagues described him as a genius and a jerk, because he was brilliant but utterly unreasonable in his demands. Jobs has many imitators: they copy the jerk easily, but find being a genius harder.

The world is not changed by reasonable people

Many successful entrepreneurs fail to realize that what they are doing is meant to be impossible, and yet they succeed. No reasonable person would take on the entire world auto industry, with its deep expertise, cost advantages and established networks. Elon Musk has already helped to change the direction of the industry. He is winning and few people would dare to call him reasonable.

Despite this, the entire management industry works on the basis that management is reasonable. Wait by the water cooler for a few minutes and you will discover the truth. All the gossip reflects a world which is intensely political and emotional, but business training misses this completely. The aptly named MBA is genuinely a Masters of Business Administration: you learn the reasonable and rational processes which you need to administer a business but you are certainly not taught to be unreasonable. This is an error as large as the error that economics made when it assumed that people are rational actors: economics is now adjusting, and business needs to adjust as well.

Reasonable managers are not in danger of over-achieving. A reasonable manager will listen to the arguments about why a new idea is too risky and might fail: new ideas and progress are killed. A reasonable manager understands when circumstances change and will extend a deadline or reduce a target: being reasonable bakes in lower performance. Reasonable managers understand why difficult decisions cannot be made. They listen to excuses and if they are reasonable, they accept them. That is the high road to mediocrity.

Being reasonable may work most of the time, but lets you down at moments of truth. Your destiny is not decided when the regular routines are working: that is when you can be reasonable. Your destiny is decided at moments of truth, when you have to step up or step back.

You face two unreasonable challenges here:

- When should you be unreasonable?
- How can you discover your ruthless streak?

The solution

When should you be unreasonable?

Leaders who are unreasonable to everyone all the time are probably psychopaths and are toxic managers. Assume that you should be reasonable 95 per cent of the time, but there are moments when you need to be unreasonable.

The times to be unreasonable are when your vision, your goal, is at risk. If your goal is important, you will do what it takes to achieve it. Key moments of truth are normally around budgets, people and setbacks or crises, as below:

Moment of truth	Reasonable managers	Unreasonable leaders
Setting next year's goals	Tweak last year's goals, plus or minus a bit: business as usual	Challenge and stretch the organization: force change and business not as usual
Negotiating your budget for next year	Follow the corporate planning process	Play hard ball, hustle and get the budget you want
Dealing with setbacks	Listen to the reasons and adjust expectations accordingly	Refuse to adjust expectations: focus only on how to get back on track
Dealing with low performers	Follow the (slow) HR process	Refuse to bring average performers on your team Help them at first, but be ready to move them out fast: the mission is more important than the individual
Bureaucratic and political obstructions	Follow the process and ask for help	Bypass the formal processes; work the politics and force a decision

Being unreasonable, even ruthless, at moments of truth is not about being nasty. It is about commitment to achieving your goal.

How can you discover your ruthless streak?
We can all be unreasonable if we have to be. If there is something you really want to achieve, you will push yourself further and harder than perhaps you thought possible. Marathon runners often hit the wall after 30–35km: they run out of energy and end up crossing the finishing line on willpower alone. All athletes learn to push themselves to an extreme in pursuit of that precious gold medal. It is easier to be unreasonable with ourselves than it is to be ruthless with colleagues. But successful leaders discover an awkward truth: the mission is more important than the individual. Collective survival is more important than individual survival.

The mission is more important than the individual

The triumph of the mission and the collective over the individual is seen clearly in schools. Most head teachers are both nice and reasonable people, despite children's perceptions. But the best head teachers also have a ruthless streak: they move out low-performing teachers fast. They do this not because they are nasty, but because there is a moral imperative to serve the children well. One bad teacher can mess up the education and future lives of over 100 children each year. Which comes first: 100 children's futures or one adult's career? Once you have real commitment to an important goal, even the most reasonable people discover that they have a ruthless streak.

9

Manage your energy: avoid burnout and stress

The challenge

Managing your energy matters for your performance and for your wellbeing.

Performance

If some staff turned up in the office drunk, they would be fired. If others stayed in the office working all night, many firms would praise them. The reaction times of the drunks and the sleep deprived are equally bad. Countless studies show that tiredness impairs judgement and performance. Drunk driving is clearly dangerous, but around 25 per cent of fatal accidents have an equally dangerous cause: tiredness. Working until you are exhausted looks heroic but is a good way to perform poorly. You can be so tired that you do not realize that you are performing poorly. Would you want to be operated on by a surgeon who has been working for 20 hours without a break?

Wellbeing

There is a quiet epidemic of stress and long hours among professionals. Stress is twice as common among people working 60 hours a week than among people working 30 hours a week. More work means more stress. This is hurting professionals, high earners and the highly qualified the most. Since the start of this century, working hours for the highest paid have been rising, while they have been falling for the lower paid. In the nineteenth century the masses toiled and the rich were idle: the twenty-first century is reversing that.

Tiredness impairs judgement and performance

The challenge is that long work hours are institutionalized in some industries. Investment banking, top law firms and consulting firms all make long hours a rite of passage for new graduates. Long hours cause many to leave, which is fine for their employers because they do not have enough space at the top to promote everyone. It is survival of the least exhausted. High divorce rates indicate that the long hours never dissipate completely. Telling people to work fewer hours simply does not work in these industries: if you want to work less, find somewhere else to work.

One way or the other, you need to find a way of managing your energy. As a leader, you have to go the extra mile at least some of the time, if not all the time.

The solution

The ideal solution is to work less, but that is not always realistic for most leaders. The imperfect but practical solution is to focus on boundaries and breaks.

The importance of boundaries and breaks was discovered over 100 years ago by FW Taylor, the founder of Scientific Management and time and motion studies. He was the #1 enemy of workers at the time, because he made it his mission to maximize the output of every worker in every shift. In one classic experiment, he got workers to increase the amount of pig iron they moved in every shift six fold. One of his key techniques was to force the workers to rest for five minutes every hour, even if they did not feel tired. He was not trying to be nice to the workers: he wanted them to work better. If you want to increase your output in the office six fold, take short breaks. Office work is mental work which means you have to be at your best all the time. Rest is not for wimps, it is for performance.

Rest is not for wimps

Here is how you can create boundaries and breaks which will give you the vital rest you need to replenish your energy reserves:

Separate home and office

When you work, really work. When you rest, really rest. It is better to stay late in the office than to take the burdens of the office back home and to keep on checking email through the night. This matters even more if you are working from home. The danger is that when you work from home, you never leave work. Create routines to mark the start and the end of the day:

some people even recreate their commute by walking round the block or to the coffee shop at the start and end of the day. If you can, create a separate work space. If you create boundaries between work and home you create the chance of having a break and resting. If you have no boundaries, you have no breaks and no rest.

Create boundaries and breaks between meetings
Zoom meetings which last one hour mean you end up with no break between meetings: you click straight from one meeting to the next. Some firms now ban one-hour meetings and insist on 50-minute meetings instead. If you cannot complete your meeting in 50 minutes, there is something wrong with the meeting. That ten-minute break allows you to recreate the natural space that happens between meetings in the office. In the office, you normally get a few minutes walking between meetings: you can grab a coffee, chat to a colleague, go to the rest room, decompress from the last meeting and mentally prepare for the next one. It turns out that breaks between meetings are not lost frictional time: they are some of the most useful time you will have in the day

Create boundaries between tasks
Break large tasks into small chunks. I wouldn't be able to write an entire book in one sitting. But I can write one section in a sitting. This is classic short interval scheduling: focus on one small task at a time. Then reward yourself with a quick break: take five minutes off to grab that coffee, walk to the water cooler, check social media. This approach helps you keep your energy up and it helps you keep on track: each small task is another way marker that you pass on your journey to completing the larger task. Short-term goal focus keeps you honest and breaks huge tasks down into manageable bite-sized chunks. This is also an effective form of time management (see chapter 10).

Create a boundary between yourself and work
It is easy to let work define who you are. Work gives structure, meaning and purpose to life. But it is easy to become dependent on work, not just financially but also socially and emotionally. You need a life outside work to help you gain perspective, and to help you stay fresh. Family is not a burden, it is a support for you. And many top leaders have strong interests outside work: Bill Gates and Warren Buffett play bridge, Richard Branson plays

chess and Alphabet CEO Sundar Pichai is a cricket fan (and attempts to play it as well, sometimes). When work is all you have, you become dependent on it and you are very vulnerable when adversity strikes.

You need a life outside work

Creating boundaries and breaks is about sustaining your energy, and avoiding burnout. But everyone pushes too far sometimes. At that point, you need a complete break: a good holiday will refresh and revive. The mistake is to think that by throttling back from 14-hour days to 12-hour days you can somehow recover. Athletes do not recover from a match by immediately playing another shorter match: they recover by resting and you need to do the same. When you need to recover, focus on recovering properly: you can decide whether that means daily ice baths or not.

As a leader you have to be intentional and purposeful in all you do, including how you manage yourself. Do not simply keep on reacting to events and working without breaks. Focus on the tasks where you make the most difference and then be deliberate in how you manage your energy:

- When you work, really work 100 per cent
- When you rest, really rest
- When you need to recover, really recover

PART TWO
LEADING TASKS

10

Use time well

The challenge

It is easy to see if front-line workers are being unproductive. You can measure how fast the production line goes, and you can measure how many deliveries the postal worker or delivery driver makes. It is far harder to measure productivity in the office, because office work is too varied and too ambiguous.

The good news is that office work appears to be chronically unproductive. A short look around most offices will reveal that many people are not on task 24/7. The US Bureau of Labor Statistics investigated office productivity and found that the average office worker was productive for a grand total of 2 hours and 58 minutes every day. Heroically, they assumed that meeting time was productive time. The rest of the time was spent on social media, making personal arrangements (shopping, travel etc.) online, chatting, having lunch and other breaks.

The advent of hybrid working showed that the office is not vital for productivity. Most firms reported that productivity was not affected by the shift to WFH (working from home), which is why most firms are happy that hybrid working is the new normal.

Never mistake activity for achievement

Low productivity is good news because it makes it easier to stand out against your peers. You do not need to work all day and all night. You simply need to work better than your colleagues.

The solution

The solution is not to work longer or to multi-task. Studies show that multi-tasking leads to doing two jobs badly. For simple confirmation of this, watch someone trying to walk and text at the same time. And if someone is trying to text and drive at the same time, they are an accident waiting to happen. Here are three ways you can work better, not harder:

1. Do the right thing

Never mistake activity for achievement. Compare the multi-tasking executive who is a whirl of activity with Charles Darwin. Darwin was a gentleman scientist who appeared to do nothing very much at all. He spent years going around the world on HMS *Beagle*, visiting friends of friends and doing his amateur science. After 20 years of pottering around, he was nudged into publishing something. *Origin of Species* then changed how we viewed the world forever. Meanwhile the busy executive is still whirling and still multi-tasking and is destined to be forgotten.

You do not need to change the world, but you do need to make sure you have something to show for your work. Have a clear goal. As a leader, you have to take people where they would not have got by themselves. Focus on where you will make a difference to your team or business. You still have to deal with all the day-to-day noise of business, but that is administration not leadership.

Don't let the urgent squeeze out the important

Be clear about your main goal for this year, this quarter, this month, this week, today and for the next hour. Don't let the urgent squeeze out the important. There are always urgent matters to attend to and they can consume your whole day. Make sure you have time to do what is important as well.

2. Avoid distractions

Distractions kill productivity. A study of coders showed that each interruption cost them 15 minutes of lost productivity, and caused them to be more error prone. If they got interrupted just twice an hour by a colleague offering a coffee or chatting about last night's TV, that is half the day lost to interruptions.

Make the most of hybrid working, if you can. You can control your home environment more than you can control the office. You have a chance to minimize interruptions at home, which makes home the ideal place for high-concentration work: writing reports, doing research, reviewing documents. The office is a less controlled environment and is more prone to interruptions, which makes it ideal for meetings and more collaborative work.

The simple message is this: when you work, work. Distractions steal your time, which you will never get back.

3. Use short interval scheduling

All the evidence shows that you cannot work well non-stop all day. You may look heroic if you work all night in the office, but such heroism is completely pointless. Both productivity and quality decline markedly with tiredness.

Target having a highly productive 25 minutes or 50 minutes, and then give yourself a break. Set yourself a clear goal for what you will achieve in that time, and then reward yourself: fix yourself a coffee, check out social media, go for a short walk. Research shows that these short breaks help you sustain maximum energy and productivity across the whole day.

By breaking the day down into a series of short-term sprints you will be able to see, and measure, the progress you make. Seeing your progress is, by itself, more motivational than randomly reacting to all the noise of the day. Inevitably, some sprints will be dealing with noise ('clear my emails, file my expenses' etc.). But some sprints should also help you move towards your longer term and more important goals.

If you really want to maximize your productivity, there is a fourth way which is even more powerful than the first three ways combined: delegate. The more you delegate, the more you free up your time to focus on what really matters. The art of delegation is covered in chapter 30.

11

Meet with purpose

The challenge

The more senior you become, the more time you spend in meetings. Middle managers spend about 35 per cent of their time in meetings; senior managers spend over half their time in meetings. Much of the rest of their time is spent preparing for meetings. This means that meetings cannot be a substitute for work. They are work, and you have to make meetings work for you. Too many meetings are a waste of time, which you cannot afford to waste. Working from home has increased the challenge. It is easy to spend all day communicating, not working, when WFH.

The solution

Here are three rules for making the most of any meeting, either as a host or as an attendee. The rules are framed as three questions which you should be able to answer positively:

1. What will I contribute?
2. What will I do differently as a result of the meeting?
3. What will I learn?

Ideally, you will be able to answer all three questions positively. You should be able to answer at least one of the three questions positively if you attend a meeting. If you leave a meeting and find that you have contributed nothing, learned nothing and will not do anything differently then you have just wasted part of your day.

You should use these three rules when you decide to attend a meeting, and when you decide who should attend a meeting you are hosting.

Applying the three rules when attending a meeting
1. What will I contribute?
If you have nothing to contribute to a meeting, you should not be there. Going to 'gain exposure' to senior management is not a good idea. If you sit silently, looking dumb, in front of top managers you are not helping your career.

Check the agenda carefully before each meeting. There should be one or two items where you can or should make your mark. You may be able to

> **If you have nothing to contribute, you should not be there**

contribute an insight, a new perspective or some data. Or perhaps you need to push a priority or protect your priorities. Know in advance which battles you want to fight and where you will make a difference. You can also use an agenda item to support a colleague and make a friend. Make the meeting work for you: your personal agenda should coincide with the formal agenda, but not be dictated by it.

2. What will I do differently as a result of the meeting?
Ideally, meetings lead to action. Sometimes there will be an agenda item where you want other people to take action: perhaps you want approval for a new project or idea, or you want a change of priorities. If you leave the decision to the meeting, that is exciting and dangerous. Always use meetings to confirm a decision, not to make a decision. The meeting should be public confirmation of the agreements you have reached in private with each of the

> **Use meetings to confirm a decision, not make a decision**

stakeholders before the meeting has started. The Japanese have a word for this: 'nemawashi', building consensus in private before gaining public confirmation.

Like battles and projects, the outcomes of all successful meetings are determined before they start. Prepare well.

3. What will I learn?
If you never learn, you never grow. Meetings are a great opportunity to learn. You learn not just about what is happening in the rest of the firm; you

can also observe and learn from how your colleagues succeed or fail, and you can learn from your own performance in the meeting.

Take a few moments after each meeting to reflect on what you have learned. This is how you will stay on top of the politics of the firm, and how you will slowly build your own unique success formula of what does and does not work. See chapter 42 for how you can learn in real time.

Applying the three rules when hosting a meeting
1. What will each attendee contribute?
As the meeting host, you have to make sure that each and every attendee has a productive meeting. That means you should look at each attendee and make sure that they can contribute something, learn something or do something different as a result of the meeting. If they can't pass these three tests, they should not be at the meeting. Let each attendee know in advance where they are expected to contribute, and where you need their support for a decision. Preparation is vital.

2. What will I be able to do differently as a result of the meeting?
Be clear about what you want to achieve in the meeting. Even a routine meeting should have an outcome. If there are six agenda items, five may be mundane but one may be an opportunity or threat for you. Focus on that one agenda item. Make sure you have prepared properly so that you get the outcome you want. Make sure the right people are in the room to make the right decision for you. Don't leave big decisions to chance. Do your 'nemawashi'.

Outcome focus helps you plan the agenda and timings. Give the most important agenda item the time it deserves. Then squeeze the routine items into any time left available. Don't let the routine squeeze out the important.

3. What will I learn?
Always debrief after a meeting with one or two trusted colleagues. As host, you will have been focused on running the meeting, so you will have seen things differently from your colleagues. You need their eyes and ears to help you on substance and process. On substance they can help you de-code what agendas were being pushed or hidden. On process they can help you take stock of what went well and what could be even better next time.

12

Talk to persuade

The challenge

All leaders are sales people. The more senior you become, the more you become a sales person. As a junior, you are told what to do. But as you take on more responsibility, you find you spend more and more of your time persuading other people to act on your word, to follow your agenda and to support your priorities. You become a sales person. This transition is explicit in professional services firms where they typically have three levels of employee, informally:

- Grinders
- Minders
- Finders

Grinders are junior staff who do the analytical work, be it auditing, legal document reviews or research for a report. Successful grinders become minders who manage the work of grinders. A few successful minders make it to Valhalla, when they are made partners. At that point they become finders or sales people. They become responsible for client development and revenue generation.

All leaders are sales people

Being a sales person is often seen as grubby, even by sales people who prefer euphemisms such as Client Relationship Manager, Business Development Executive or Partner. But wherever you are in the organization, you have to master the art of selling your idea, selling your point of view. To make this more respectable, we can call it being persuasive.

If you want to succeed as a leader, you have to learn to be persuasive.

The solution

If you dislike the idea of selling, do not worry. Hopefully, you like having conversations. Selling is nothing more than a structured conversation which is persuasive. The persuasive conversation has two vital principles and one simple process.

Two principles of persuasion
1. Two ears and one mouth
To be persuasive you need some basic physical characteristics: you need two ears and one mouth. And you need to use them in that proportion. You need to listen at least twice as much as you talk. The best persuaders are not the best talkers: they are the best listeners.

Listening is not about waiting to make your point

Listening is your secret weapon. When you listen you discover what the other person really wants, needs and fears. You can tailor your message to what they want to hear. Listening is also flattering and a good way of building trust and rapport. In a time-starved world, you flatter someone by investing time in listening to their views. So listening does two vital things for you:

- You understand the other person's agenda and can adjust accordingly
- You start to win a friend, which is the first step to winning the argument

Listening is not about waiting to make your point while ignoring what they say. It is active listening, so that you understand their views properly. The test of active listening is to paraphrase, or summarize, what they have just said. Paraphrasing is a powerful technique because:

- It forces you to listen and understand
- It avoids misunderstanding: if you summarize what was just said incorrectly, you quickly find out and can fix the problem
- It builds rapport by showing to the other person you really understand them
- It shuts up anxious people who often repeat their point over and over again, because they think they have not been heard or understood. Paraphrasing their point back to them assures them that they have been heard, and they can relax.

Normally, it is very easy to get people to talk because people like hearing their favourite sound: themselves. If necessary, nudge them with an open question. Open questions are ones which cannot be answered 'yes' or 'no', and will often start with a how, why, what or possibly when.

2. The partnership principle

Selling can be an adversarial win/lose transaction: think of buying a second-hand car. Far better is to build a win/win relationship in which you act as partners to each other. You both need each other, and you have to work out how best to help each other. Even, or especially, if you are dealing with a very important person you should apply the partnership principle. You are not asking for a favour or offering a favour: you are working together to help each other. Act as an equal. If you act as a supplicant or as a salesperson, that is how you will be treated and it will be hard to have a good conversation.

Think of yourself as a partner, not as an adversary, supplicant or salesperson. In other words, act and behave as you normally would with any of your colleagues. Then you can use the structure of the persuasive conversation to achieve your goal.

The process of persuasion: the persuasive conversation

A persuasive conversation is simply a normal conversation with a structure, where you aim to listen more than talk. The structure has seven steps, summarized by the acronym PASSION. Think of each step of the PASSION process as a set of traffic lights. Do not proceed to the next step until the lights turn green. The process can take less than a minute if you are persuading a trusted colleague to do you a simple favour. It can take years if you are selling a fleet of aircraft to an airline. The basic structure of the PASSION process is always the same. PASSION stands for:

- Preparation
- Alignment
- Situation
- Size the prize
- Idea
- Objections overcome
- Next steps

Here is how it works:

1. Preparation

Understand as much as you can about what your counter party wants, needs and fears. The fatal mistake is to fall in love with your own idea. You may love your idea, but how will the other person see it? Your new initiative may look like it will seal your bonus or promotion, but to others it may look like extra work, risk and distraction from their priorities. See the world through the eyes of others, not just yourself.

Preparation is also about the basics:

- When are we going to meet and what expectations should I set beforehand?
- Where will we meet, and what sort of atmosphere do I want to create?
- Who should be at the meeting? As soon as you meet with more than one person, the meeting becomes public and people start to take positions: it becomes much harder to have a persuasive conversation.
- What collateral (samples, slides etc.) do we need? Often no collateral is best. How often do you see heads of government persuading each other at a summit with a PowerPoint presentation? Collateral creates an 'us and them' barrier and turns you from being a partner to being a salesperson.

2. Alignment

Alignment is both professional and personal.

Personal alignment matters because it is easier to persuade a friend than to persuade a foe. We find it easier to trust people who are like ourselves. That means it helps if you can find common ground. This may be shared interests, shared background, conferences you have both been to, or holidays you have in common. Background preparation helps. Check out the social media profile and formal publications of the person you will meet. You will probably find something of common interest, or at least a starting point for a conversation. Failing that, look at the office or Zoom background of the other person. Normally, there will be some personal items on display which can help you find a common interest.

It is easier to persuade a friend than to persuade a foe

Professional alignment is about showing you both share similar goals and similar values. If you are chasing your agenda at their expense you set up a win/lose argument. It will not be pretty or pleasant. To discover how your goals align, you need to proceed to the next stage of the conversation: the situation.

The best way to build alignment is to listen. Asking smart questions is better than making smart points.

3. Situation

This is where you go into listening overdrive. Resist the temptation to extol the brilliance of your idea. Brilliance is in the eye of the beholder. Understand how others will see your idea. Your goal here is to understand how your idea fits with the wants, needs and fears of the other person.

What people want is not always what they say. For instance, buyers often want to negotiate hard on price. But other things matter as well: reliability, service, lifetime cost versus initial cost, effect on profitability and so on. Ask questions to find out what really matters from their perspective. This gives you the ammunition you need to pitch your idea successfully.

What people want is not always what they say

This part of the conversation is often the longest, and most creative. You are mentally drawing a Venn diagram of their world and yours. You want to discover the segment where your two worlds overlap: that is where your common interest lies.

You know you have completed this part of the conversation when you can summarize it like this: 'so if I understand you correctly, if we can find a way of achieving X, that would be helpful?' You will not have stated your idea, yet. But you will know that your idea is a great way of helping to achieve X. In essence, you will have nearly sold your idea without actually describing it.

4. Size the prize

This is where you articulate the 'WIFM' factor: 'What's In it For Me?' You may have a great idea to save the world, but you have to make it relevant to the person you are talking with. Articulate the benefits of your idea, from their perspective. This is where you will find yourself saying something like: 'so if we work on this together the result will be ... prize Y'. If the prize is big, relevant and credible then the other person will be very keen to hear your idea.

The prize comes in several flavours:

- Financial prizes are always compelling. 'This will save us $5 million per year.' No one wants to be the klutz that stands in the way of saving $5 million per year.
- Non-financial prizes can also be strong if you can quantify them: 'this will reduce our time to market by one month/ this will reduce employee attrition by 15 per cent'. In practice, you normally find that you can show the financial benefit of such non-financial prizes.
- Qualitative prizes are often attractive, but weak: 'this will improve our market profile/we will be more attractive to potential recruits'.

If in doubt, try to quantify the financial benefits of your non-financial or qualitative idea. Money talks.

5. Idea

By the time you state your idea, the other person should already be wanting to hear it and to agree to it. As you describe your idea, take the opportunity to pre-empt any objections that may arise such as: 'it is too expensive, too risky, too much work'. A good way to do this is to recognize the problem explicitly and then tell a story, which can sound like this: 'When I was discussing this idea with my colleagues/boss/team earlier they were concerned that it would cost too much. And of course the initial cost is high. But then they realized that the lifetime cost would be much lower and it would lead to big cost savings elsewhere....'

6. Objections

The best way to deal with objections is to pre-empt them. If you have listened well, you will know what objections the other person will have.

The next best way to deal with objections is to agree with them, and then invite the other person to find a solution with you. If you have established a partnership working style, they will help you find the solution. If you act as a salesperson or supplicant, they will act as judge and jury. That will not be to your benefit.

Your colleagues are not mind readers

The worst way to deal with an objection is to argue about it. As soon as you start arguing, you lose. Even if you are right, the other person will not want to accept that they are wrong. If you find the objections are flowing fast and furious, then something has gone wrong earlier in the conversation. Normally, the problem will be that you have not understood the situation properly. At this point, stop arguing and go back to understanding the situation: listen and ask smart questions.

7. Next steps

Fortunately, your colleagues are not mind readers. You need to be clear about what happens next. In selling terms, you need to 'close' the conversation. Here are some classic ways of closing the conversation:

- The direct close: 'Do you agree to the plan to buy 100 laptops?' This is powerful, but dangerous because it opens up the possibility of 'no', at which point you have to start all over again.
- The action close: 'I will raise the purchase order for you to authorize.' This has the virtue of making 'no' a difficult response.
- The assumed close: 'so we are all agreed that we will buy 100 pink and yellow laptops....' It takes some bravery to step up and argue against the assumed close.
- The alternate close: 'Would you like us to buy the pink laptops or the yellow ones?' This does not allow for 'no'. It is often used by consultants who offer three courses of action: the cheap and useless option, the expensive and unaffordable option and the option they want you to agree to. You give people the illusion of making a decision and taking ownership, but in practice you are only letting them agree with what you want.

At this stage, you may discover one more vital element of the preparation phase: always have a Plan B. If the conversation goes awry, you need to be ready with a close which enables some form of progress. This may be to agree a further meeting, or to agree to a modified form of your idea. It is far easier to do this if you have prepared a Plan B than if you try to make it up on the spur of the moment.

13

Present to persuade

The challenge

Presenting is a challenge for three reasons:

- Many people fear it
- Presenting has a disproportionate effect on your career
- The quality of many presentations is very low

Fear of presenting

Enough people fear speaking in public that it has its own name: glossophobia (ancient Greek: *glossa* for tongue and *phobos* for fear). A survey by Chapman University found that more Americans feared public speaking than feared heights, bugs and snakes, blood and needles, or even ghosts and clowns. That fear is real: the sweaty palms, the breathlessness, feeling unable to speak or to think clearly. That is not good for you or your career.

Importance of presenting

Presenting is your moment in the spotlight, and it is the moment you will be judged by your peers and bosses. Overtly, they will react to the content of your presentation. Covertly they will be reacting to you. It is your chance to sell yourself and accelerate your career.

Quality of presenting

Think back on the last few presentations you went to. How many were of high quality and value in terms of impact and enjoyment? Even the most useful presentations tend to be endured, not enjoyed. Weak presentations are death by bullet point, which is cruel in the extreme. This is good news for you. By presenting well, you will stand out in a sea of mediocrity. It is your chance to shine.

This section will deal with the fear and quality of presenting in terms of substance and style.

Weak presentations are death by bullet point

The solutions

You do not have to learn to be a brilliant orator who makes a fortune on the speaking circuit, although that could turn out to be a rewarding side hustle. You need to stand out against your peers. That is a low hurdle to jump, so make the most of it. To shine, you need to do three things:

1. Overcome the fear of presenting
2. Develop an effective style of presenting
3. Have strong substance and structure in your presentation

1. Overcome the fear of presenting

You can acquire the courage to present in the same way as you acquire any other sort of courage (see chapter 3): take incremental steps, develop expertise and keep on practising.

Take incremental steps. Your first presentation should not be a one-hour keynote to the entire firm. Instead, start with short talks to small groups and slowly build up. A good initial exercise is to ask three or four close colleagues to talk for three minutes about their best, or most vivid or most exciting thing that happened to them in the last year. This is safe (because of the group) and easy (because of the topic). As you talk about the memorable event, you will find you display the strengths of the best speakers: you will have the three Es of energy, excitement and enthusiasm. Never lose those three Es.

Develop expertise. The more you know your topic, the more you will feel in control. You will feel confident about answering questions.

Keep on practising. Practise makes perfect and generates confidence. As far as possible, replicate the actual event in advance. If you cannot use the facilities before the event, visualize it in detail: what it will look like, the sounds, the lighting, even the smells. Visualizing success is a vital tool for many sports people. The more realistic it is, the more you will feel comfortable on the day itself: you will be in familiar, not unfamiliar territory.

2. Develop an effective style of presenting

Think back on all the presentations you have been to. You will probably struggle to remember much of the detail from a presentation six months ago. But you will have vivid memories of what the presenter was like. You will remember the style (presenter) better than you remember the substance (presentation). Some presentations are death by bullet point, with a boring presenter droning on endlessly. Other presentations are engaging and energizing, and you probably judge both the presentation and the presenter positively.

If you want to be remembered well, focus on the three Es of the best presenters: energy, excitement and enthusiasm. Although enthusiasm is a certifiable disease in some organizations, it is a good way to engage your audience. Your three Es will be enabled by a fourth: expertise. It is easier to be enthusiastic when you know what you are talking about and believe in it.

3. Have strong substance and structure in your presentation

A good presentation is like a good document: it is complete not when you can say no more; it is complete when you can say no less. Cut the presentation down to the minimum of what you need to say, not what you want to say. You can achieve focus by answering one question: 'who am I trying to persuade to do what?' Once you are clear about that, try writing a newspaper headline which summarizes your entire presentation: use ten

You want dumb slides and a smart presenter

words or less. This is a tough discipline, but once you have your headline you have your focus. Then identify the minimum you need to make your case. Suddenly, huge amounts of material can disappear into back-up material where they can be used to answer any questions. Your presentation will be crisp, focused and compelling.

At the margins, a few simple tricks help with both substance and style:

- *Learn your opening by heart*, and make it a good opening. No matter how nervous you are, this lets you start well. Once you have started well it is easy to carry on.
- *Use simple slides.* You want dumb slides and a smart presenter, not the other way around. The slides should do no more than help the audience keep track of where you are. The nightmare is to have smart slides and a dumb presenter: the slides say everything and the presenter simply reads the slides.

- *Learn some memorable phrases,* facts or views which will catch attention. Each memorable moment acts as a useful waymarker for you in your presentation and will summarize the key point you want to make.
- *Have a good finish,* which you also can learn by heart. If you start well and end well you have captured the moments which you will be remembered by most easily. Asking 'any questions?' at the end is feeble. End with a call to action, a challenge or present a vivid choice to be made.
- *Get help.* Ask your colleagues to help you perfect your presentation: they will be more objective than you. Get help from other stakeholders to understand what is really expected from the presentation and what 'good' looks like. Get professional help if you want to improve your style and substance. Learning by trial and error is painful, and a professional can accelerate your learning and minimize your pain.

14

Write with impact

The challenge

You probably suffer from reading too many boring reports and emails, which are jargon filled and badly written. There is plenty of evidence that our colleagues cannot write well. The problem is that we are all someone's colleague. They may rate your writing the same way you rate theirs.

As a leader, you do not need to write as well as Shakespeare, but you do need to write for impact. Even a routine report should tell a story and lead the reader to think or act differently. **Good writing is a sign of good thinking** How you write sets the standard for your team. If you are verbose and riddled with jargon, do not expect your team to write crisply, clearly and with insight. Good writing is always a sign of good thinking; force yourself and your team to write clearly, and you force everyone to think clearly.

The solution

The first editor I worked with had five simple rules of writing. He always caught me out with these rules, and I still struggle to follow them all the time.

1. *Write for the reader.* Writing is not a vanity exercise where you impress yourself. You need to engage your reader. What is it she needs or wants to read? Focus relentlessly on her and you will find clarity in your message. If you are writing for a group, there will usually be one or two people you most need to focus on. Focus on them and you will sharpen your message.

2. *Tell a story.* Work out the headline, which should be as short as a newspaper headline. Then everything else should be organized to support that headline. This will give your document coherence, focus and brevity. You will be able to cut out vast amounts of excess information.

3. *Support assertions with facts.* One unsupported assertion or incorrect fact undermines the credibility of the entire document. Be suspicious of power adjectives. If you say something is important (or 'strategic', which is important with bells on) show why it is important for your reader. If it is only important for you, that is your problem.

4. *Make it active.* Avoid the passive, negative and conditional forms. Being passive or negative is not business like. The conditional form conveys uncertainty, not confidence. Use positive words and positive language if you want to be seen as positive. Write the way you want to be seen.

5. *Keep it short and simple.* Documents are like diamonds: they benefit from good cutting. You can summarise any report, problem or plan in less than one page. Also, keep each sentence and each word short. Twelve words per sentence is an ideal, but tough, goal. Long words impress the writer, not the reader.

These disciplines will not only help you write clearly: they will help you think clearly.

15

Read (and listen) with purpose

The challenge

The challenge is that you are reading this. So why should you read about how to read?

In practice, reading for business is different from reading for pleasure. When you are reading for pleasure you can be led by the author. If the author is any good, you will be surprised, delighted, amused or enlightened by the thoughts which the author creates in your mind. You can afford to be reactive. In business you can never afford to be reactive. You need to be a critical reader.

In business you can never afford to be reactive

The solution

There are three keys to the arcane art of reading for business. You can use these keys to become a much better business reader. You can also use them to become much more critical and insightful when attending meetings. These are simple but powerful keys to master. Here they are:

1. *Decide on your point of view before reading the document*, or listening to the presentation or attending a meeting. Do not just pick up the document and start reading, and do not just turn up to the presentation and start listening. If you do that, you will be reactive and you will let your head be filled with the thoughts of the writer: the smarter the writer, the harder it is to escape the internal logic which they present you with.

By having a point of view beforehand, you become a critical reader. When you read with prejudice, you quickly spot the assertions and assumptions which need to be challenged. You do not get trapped by the brilliant internal logic in front of you.

2. *Make a list of topics you expect the document or presentation to cover,* before you start. This allows you to achieve the impossible: you can spot the invisible. You see what is not there. When something is missing, there is normally a bad reason why it is missing: it may well not support the argument being presented. If there is nothing on the competition, or the financial data is minimal, you should notice that and be ready to interrogate the competitive or financial data in detail.

3. *Debrief with colleagues.* However good you are at reading and listening, your colleagues will inevitably hear and see different things. Even if they hear the same things, they will react in different ways because they have different priorities, agendas and skills. They will be filtering the information through a different lens and come to different conclusions. The more important the document or presentation, the more important it is to debrief.

16

Work the numbers

The challenge

Some people love numbers, spreadsheets and financial analysis. Many people feel slightly intimidated by them. Both sets of people make the same mistake: they think that financial analysis and spreadsheets are about the numbers. Insight does not come from complex calculations worked out to six decimal points. Insight comes from understanding the assumptions which lie behind the numbers.

Clearly, accurate numbers matter. Spreadsheets simplify the process of calculation. But the calculation is only as good as the assumptions which lie behind the numbers. Working the numbers matters, but working the assumptions matters even more.

Working the numbers matters, but working the assumptions matters even more

The challenge is most often seen in the bottom right-hand corner of the spreadsheet. This is where 'the answer' appears. You can be assured that if the target is $x million profit or x per cent return on equity, then the answer in the bottom right-hand corner will be x, plus a little bit for safety. The spreadsheet has been developed from the bottom right-hand corner backwards. Assumptions have been tweaked and adjusted to make the right answer magically appear in the bottom right-hand corner of the spreadsheet. Do not waste time challenging the calculations, because the spreadsheet should do that well. Spend your time challenging the assumptions.

Spreadsheets and financial analysis are about clear thinking and testing assumptions first and foremost.

The solution

When working with numbers, you should keep in mind three sorts of questions:

The venture capitalist's questions

Venture capitalists see endless proposals which promise to change the world and make them rich. They have to sort the best from the rest, and working the details of each proposal is more or less impossible: that requires too much time and expertise understanding the details of each new or existing market. Instead, they have a simple short cut for screening proposals. They ask: 'who is behind this proposal?'

A proposal from an unknown person who has no track record is far riskier than a proposal from a successful entrepreneur with a good track record. The same applies within the firm. A proposal from a manager with an A* record of making things happen is far more likely to succeed than a proposal from someone with a weak track record or no track record.

You can use this to your advantage when preparing a proposal. If you have limited track record, find an executive who has a very good track record and enlist his or her support. The chances are that they will be demanding: they will push you hard to shape the proposal, build the evidence and gain support. The end result will not only be rationally stronger, it will also be politically far stronger. It will have immediate credibility with other top managers because of the credibility of the person who is sponsoring the proposal for you.

The banker's questions

Spreadsheets and financial analysis usually lie because they usually predict a single point outcome. Real life is never so certain. In practice, a range of outcomes is likely depending on whether the more optimistic or pessimistic scenarios play out in the future. This is where we leap into the land of the 'what if' question: these challenge assumptions and create plausible scenarios for you to test.

Start with the big assumptions: market size and growth, pricing and margins, key cost inputs. For example, in one life insurance business assuming interest rates increased or decreased by 1 per cent was enough to shift a product from being wildly profitable to being extremely unprofitable.

Do not worry about the cost of office laptops, unless you are in the business of selling office laptops. Focus on what matters, not on what is easy.

If you are preparing a proposal you may be asked to present a single point solution. But you should still prepare different scenarios with different assumptions. This will enable you to answer the 'what if' questions, and will also help you identify the critical assumptions on which your proposal depends.

Knowing which numbers to test often comes down to the next set of questions: the manager's questions.

The manager's questions

In every business there are the sacred and serious numbers which everyone tracks to monitor the health of the business. At the firm wide level, these might be occupancy rates (hotels), average yield per passenger mile and load factor (airlines), number of eyeballs (endless internet start-ups), market share (many FMCG products). Below the firm level, each business unit and department will have its own vital statistics which are monitored closely.

As a leader and manager you will be familiar with the sacred and serious numbers which matter for your business. You should test any financial proposal or spreadsheet against those numbers. If you see a number which looks implausibly high or low, you need to start digging. You will probably find a faulty assumption. An implausible number may also be a symptom of a complex formula which has been constructed incorrectly for the spreadsheet. You do not need to analyse the formula yourself: you simply need to see that there is a problem and then find a spreadsheet genius to fix it.

PART THREE

LEADING PEOPLE

17

Set goals

The challenge

Goal setting in the days of command and control was easy. The job of the manager was to pass orders down the hierarchy and to pass information back up it. You told the team what to do, and possibly how to do it, and then monitored them to make sure they did it. This ensured compliance, which is all that the organization required.

Goal setting today is much harder, for two reasons: ambiguity and ownership.

Ambiguity

Professional work is ambiguous. If you are asked to write a report, it could be one page or 100 pages long. But however long it is, there will always be another fact you could check or another opinion you could seek. It is not like making widgets where you can specify and measure both the quantity and quality you want. The ambiguity of professional work makes it hard to specify everything you want on a piece of paper or in an email. But if you let the ambiguity persist, the result will be redundant effort, rework and loss of morale.

Ownership

You need your team to take ownership of the goal for you. If the goal is seen as 'your' goal, your team will have low interest in making it work. They may even be happy to sabotage it passively, to prove that you are wrong. They will delegate every problem back up to you: that is a recipe for over-work, under-performance and stress. If they see it as 'their' goal they will

Building ownership is about persuasion, not instruction

be committed to making it work and will find ways of dealing with all the challenges which any course of action entails. Your challenge is to transfer ownership of the goal from you to them. Building ownership is about persuasion, not instruction.

The solution

Here are two ways to solve the ambiguity challenge, and one way to deal with the ownership challenge.

Ambiguity (1): SMART goals

SMART is a useful acronym to remember in setting goals which should be Specific, Measurable, Achievable, Relevant and Time Bound. The acronym is explained below, using an example where the goal is to deliver a workshop.

- Specific. This is where you answer the 'W' questions: what is required, who for, when, where and why. A one-hour workshop for the board, delivered remotely, will be very different from a two-day workshop for 30 people at a conference centre.
- Measurable. Here you have to answer the question 'how will I know if it has succeeded?' Do not confuse outputs with outcomes. The output is that the workshop was delivered, which is easy to measure. The outcome is harder to measure but more important: what has changed as a result of the workshop? Have new skills been acquired, have behaviours (such as teamwork) changed? Find a measurable output and that will help you focus your efforts.
- Achievable. This is a good moment to ask 'how do we set this up for success?' You need to make sure that you have the right resources, people, skills, budget and support in place to ensure the workshop succeeds. There is no point in setting a goal unless you invest in making it succeed. If it is not worth investing in the goal, it is not worth setting the goal.
- Relevant. This is your chance to explore whether the goal really matters at all by asking questions like: 'who needs this?', 'why does it matter to them?', 'how does this fit with all our other priorities?'

If the workshop does not really matter to the potential attendees, you will find that either they do not turn up, or they turn up but do not engage.

- Time bound. A goal with no deadline is not a goal, it is a vague hope. The final delivery deadline for the workshop is a spur to action. But you need intermediate deadlines as well to check that you are on track and to get support if you need it. A small project plan with key deadlines and dependencies will clarify who needs to do what by when.

Ambiguity (2): move beyond 'what' to 'why'

Rookie journalists are taught that every news item should answer the 'who', 'what', 'where' and 'when' questions, but that the most interesting question is always 'why'. This should be the same mantra for all leaders. The 'why' question is embedded within SMART goals, but it is important enough that it deserves its own section.

'Why' should be the first question to ask because it is more revealing about the 'who', 'what' and 'when' questions. For instance:

- Why is this report needed? Why is it important? This leads to questions such as 'who needs it?', 'what is the problem we are solving for them?', 'why do they need it by next Friday?'
- Why do you want me to focus on this new project? Why did we choose this project out of all the other alternatives? What does a good outcome look like to whom, and why?

The purpose of these questions is to understand the context of the goal. Where work is ambiguous, context is vital to establish clarity and help your team make the right decisions about how and where to focus their effort. Your team are probably not mind readers: you need to help them understand the thought process you went through in arriving at your decision. Once the team really understands the goal, they can take ownership of it and they can proceed without having to refer back to you the whole time to ensure that they are still on track.

A goal with no deadline is a vague hope

Clarifying the context of the goal is a journey of discovery. It is more or less impossible to capture all the context and questions in a memo or email. Invest time in discussing the goal at the start to save time and effort later on.

Ownership: build commitment, not just compliance

The discovered solution is always valued more highly than the dictated solution. If you tell people what to do, that is a dictated solution which may gain grudging compliance. If your team works out what they need to do for themselves, they will be committed to that course of action and will want to make it work.

That means you need to switch from telling mode to listening mode. A simple way to switch modes is to ask good questions such as 'what do we need to do to set you up for success?' Encourage your team to air their concerns, ask questions and examine their options. This appears to be inefficient compared to the old school way of telling your team what to do and how to do it. Although inefficient, it is highly effective. The more your team discuss the goal, the more they can internalize it and own it.

18

Coach for performance

The challenge

Traditionally, the boss was meant to be the smartest person in the room. Bosses had the brains and workers had the hands: the job of the boss was to get his (it was always his) ideas out of his head and into the hands of the workers who did what they were told. If there was a problem, the boss had to fix it. All problems would be delegated up to the boss.

As a boss, you do not need to be the smartest person in the room: you need to get the smartest people into the room. If they are smart, you do not need to solve every problem for them. You have to help them solve the problem themselves. In other words, you have to coach them.

In practice, teams avoid coaching. Followers find it easier to delegate problems up to the boss, and bosses find it easier to provide the solution than to 'waste' time helping a team member find the solution. Providing the solution also feels very managerial: the old paradigm of bosses having the brains still exists. You have to challenge and change this behaviour. If every problem gets delegated up to you then:

You need to get the smartest people into the room

- You will be overloaded in terms of work. You will have less time to focus on your real priorities.
- You will be stressed out thinking about all the problems.
- Your team will never learn or grow: they will become ever more dependent on you. They will delegate upwards more and more.
- Your performance and your career will suffer.

Managers also avoid coaching because they do not know how to do it. Few managers receive training on coaching. Coaching as a manager is different from coaching as a coach. Some coaches like to answer every question with a question: that may (or may not) work for personal coaching, but does not work for managers who have to coach for performance and for results. This section gives you a simple framework for holding a productive coaching conversation.

The solution

Think of every coaching conversation as a problem solving conversation. Coaching as a manager is not about being a part-time psychotherapist or wellbeing guru. It is about helping your team member find a solution to the problem they present to you. Thinking about coaching as problem solving makes it an easier task for leaders to deal with.

Think about coaching as problem solving

The coaching conversation has five stages, which we can call the five 'O' model. The conversation can be short or long. You can use your own style and language for the conversation. All that the five 'O' model does is to give you a structure to your conversation. Use the structure and you will find you can move from a vague statement of a problem to having a team member committed to delivering a specific solution.

The five 'O' model is this:

1. Objectives
2. Overview
3. Options
4. Obstacles
5. Outcome

In practice, you will find that your team member knows the solution at least eight times out of ten: they simply need to talk it through and get reassurance that they are heading in the right direction. On these occasions, the conversation may be quick and may do no more than help the team member refine their original idea. Sometimes the team member knows the answer, but does not realize it. These conversations are genuine problem solving conversations which take more time. Perhaps one in ten times there will be a problem which neither of you know the answer to. At that point, you do not need a coaching conversation: you need help. Call a team meeting, bring in an expert as necessary. Do not try to be a hero and solve it yourself.

You are likely to encounter three categories of problem when coaching a team member:

- Rational problems: 'How can we deal with the latest 10 per cent budget cut?'
- Emotional problems: 'I am feeling really exhausted and demotivated at the moment'
- Political problems: 'I am constantly being undermined by our colleagues in finance/sales/IT etc.'

The five 'O' model applies equally to each category of problem. The problem solving approach lets you cut through the politics and emotion of a situation and drive to a solution which leads to action.

Here is how to hold your problem solving coaching conversation:

1. Objectives

From your perspective, the objective of every coaching conversation is to help your team member discover a solution which works for them. Always, the discovered solution is better than the dictated solution. If you reveal a solution to them, they will not own it. If it is their solution, they will be committed to making it happen which is what you want as a leader. There is always a risk that they will find a solution which is better than the one you think up. Live with that risk.

Note that the problem they present to you may not be the problem they need to work on. Don't worry too much about that at this stage: the next step may well reveal the real problem.

2. Overview

This is the meat of your conversation. You will do two things here.

First, you will encourage your team member to see the problem from different perspectives. For instance, a common conversation is where the team member is complaining about unreasonable behaviour from another department and does not know what to do about it. Invariably, your team member will be the saint and the other department will be the sinners. At this point, ask your team member to describe how the other department will see events. The more you push different perspectives, the more both of you will understand what is really going on. Do not accept your team member's initial narrative as the whole truth.

Second, as you listen to your team member talk, you will be thinking about solutions, or hypotheses you would like to test. This is where you can ask some more questions to gently test out potential solutions. The chances are that your team member will also be thinking about potential solutions. So when you are satisfied that you have both found a reasonably objective understanding of the situation, you can proceed to the next step.

3. Options

This is the riskiest and most rewarding part of the conversation. The risk is that you let slip your idea for a solution. At that point, the coaching conversation is over. You have revealed your solution and the team member will have little or no ownership of it. You have reverted to the traditional role of the boss being the smartest person in the room.

Let your team member come up with one or more solutions. Ask them directly: 'How could you deal with this? What other options do you have?' Do not criticize the solutions yourself: that is again playing the traditional boss role. Encourage your team member to come up with more than a single point solution. If they identify several options, then you can let them compare and evaluate the different options. You do not need to criticize an option: they will do the criticism for you.

Ideas are good, action is better As they work through each option, they will find one which they believe will work for them. Unless you know it is a bad solution, let them run with it. If they own the solution, they will be committed to making it work.

At this stage, it is tempting to declare victory and end the conversation. You have a solution, what more do you need? You need two more things.

4. Obstacles

The danger is that your team member happily disappears ... and then reappears, demotivated and confused, a few days later as they hit some unforeseen obstacle. Identify and deal with those obstacles now. At minimum, this will save you another coaching conversation later. If the obstacles are too great, you may choose to identify another solution to the problem. This short step can save both of you time and grief later on. Simple questions will tease out any problems:

- What will stop you achieving this?
- Will you need any help or support to do this?
- What obstacles/problems do you anticipate with this?

5. Outcome

Ideas are good, action is better. Don't finish the meeting open-ended. As a leader you need to make sure that a good solution leads to action. This is the moment for you to check next steps, timing and when you will receive the next update.

19

Giving feedback

The challenge

Feedback is a three-part problem:

1. Feedback is often negative. Human nature means we are attuned to threats, problems and risks. That is an ingrained survival mechanism we inherit from our ancestors. We are more likely to see and respond to threats and problems than to remark on things which are running well. Things are meant to run well, so why comment on them? Negative feedback reinforces widespread dislike of feedback, because most people do not enjoy being criticized.

2. Feedback sets up the classic adult/child relationship where the adult praises or scolds the child. As a result, most people dislike giving and receiving feedback. Professionals want to be treated as adults, not like children. Year-end school reports are not popular with children: year-end appraisals are even less popular with professionals.

3. Managers avoid giving feedback because they dislike it (see points one and two above). The result is that year-end appraisals are often surprises to the person being appraised. The year-end appraisal is transformed from a constructive process into a traumatic contest between the two sides who have different interpretations of history.

The solution

Just as feedback is a three-part problem, so it is a three-part solution. Each solution mirrors one of the problems.

Praise at least nine times out of ten

1. *Focus on positive feedback.* Some of the best managers use the 90/10 rule of feedback: praise at least nine times out of ten. There are few people who dislike being praised. Just as likes on social media create a small dopamine hit (which hooks us on to the social media site), so praise from your boss creates a major dopamine hit.

   Make praise work for you. You can do this two ways. First, be specific in your praise. Don't just say 'well done'. Be specific about what was done well and how it affected you: 'the way you dealt with that question from the client was great: I had not thought of that answer myself and it clearly made a vital difference in their decision to go with us'. That is much more powerful than 'thanks for pitching in today'.

   Second, let them relish their success. When someone comes to you with good news, don't just brush them off with a passive 'well done' while staring at your computer screen. Stop what you are doing for a moment. Focus on the good news bearer. Ask them to tell you about what they did and how they did it. This achieves two goals. You flatter when you listen to and recognize your team member. It also helps them learn, because they are identifying not just what went well but how they did it. Keep on probing with questions so that they learn more and can relish their success even more. They will learn and they will love you for it.

   Positive feedback is how your team will learn from success

   Positive feedback is how your team will learn from success. Leaders tend to treat success as normal. It is not. Whenever something goes right, it is the result of hard work and people doing something well. Make sure that they learn from each success, so that success becomes a habit.

2. *Turn the adult/child conversation into an adult-to-adult conversation.*
   Avoid criticism, because that will lead to an argument or rejection.
   Instead of telling them they messed up, ask them if they achieved
   the outcome they wanted or expected. Normally, they will then
   tell you exactly what the problem was, and where things went
   wrong and what they could do differently next time. You do not
   need to tell people these things because often they know. Let them
   structure the feedback for you. Use coaching techniques (chapter
   18) to help them explore the problem, the solution and the next
   steps. Act as their partner and coach. Turn negative feedback into
   positive learning.

   By turning feedback into coaching and turning criticism into
   learning you can create a strong version of the 90/10 rule. 90 per
   cent of the time you praise and learn, the other 10 per cent of the
   time you coach and learn. In other words, 100 per cent of the time
   you focus on learning and you criticize 0 per cent of the time.

3. *Normalize feedback.* Make it frequent and two way. Let them give
   you feedback and encourage your team to reflect on how they
   work as a team. By making feedback frequent and positive it
   becomes a habit. It also means that the year-end review becomes
   more or less irrelevant. If you cannot dispense with the year-end
   review, it will become no more than a formality: there will be no
   surprises because it will simply summarize what you have been
   discussing all year.

   If you normalize feedback fully, you create a learning team
   and organization. Your team will expect to debrief frequently
   and positively, and each individual will actively want to learn and
   improve.

20

Dealing with poor performance

The challenge

Poor performance presents two traps to the unwary leader: act too fast, act too slow.

Act too fast

Some firms still have a system where they cull the bottom 10 per cent of managers each year: 'rank and yank'. This is meant to raise the bar: only the fittest survive. In practice, it is a recipe for politics and infighting: everyone wants to hog the credit and duck the blame when things go right or wrong. It also means that many good managers get culled. Even the best managers have bad years: perhaps they got a bad assignment, they were let down by third parties or the market moved against them. Firing people and promoting people on the basis of luck is not good management.

Even where the firm does not enforce a cull, some leaders are more than happy to cull managers at the first sign of trouble. Often 'trouble' turns out to be no more than a clash of styles. This looks macho, but faces all the same problems that the systemic cull faces: losing good managers through bad luck, encouraging politics and discouraging teamwork.

Act too slow

Removing someone from your team seriously messes with their career and their life. The result is that many leaders prefer to avoid the difficult conversation until it is far too late. An early discussion about weak performance can be a constructive conversation about how to improve performance, to understand what is holding the individual back and to support your team member properly. Leaving it late means that the news is often a surprise, and it is too late to have a constructive conversation. The result is messy conflict.

Poor performance is a reality of life. Everyone goes through bad patches, and occasionally people land up in the wrong role. As a leader, you have to deal with it.

The solution

The solution is based on good housekeeping. Stick to three core disciplines and you will manage even the toughest situation:

1. Goal clarity
2. Frequent feedback
3. Spot the dip versus the doom loop

Followers, like leaders, dislike surprises

There is one big trap to avoid: the style clash. Many apparent performance problems turn out to be a clash of styles between team leader and team member. When this happens, it is easy for the team leader to make negative judgements about everything the team member does. That turns the style clash into a war, which has one inevitable outcome: the team member will either jump or be pushed. Either way, they will leave and both sides lose as a result.

1. Goal clarity

Poor performance is often disputed, because the goals were not set correctly in the first place (see chapter 17 on setting goals and chapter 30 on delegation). When you set out on a new project or task, it is human nature to proceed with goodwill. You broadly agree the goal and then trust your team member to deliver. That is like agreeing to do some building work on the basis of a handshake and goodwill. When problems arise and costs escalate, the result is an argument which has no resolution because the goals, the budget, the timing, the details were not agreed at the start.

2. Frequent feedback

Followers, like leaders, dislike surprises for the same reason: surprises are rarely good. And if you are surprised, it is too late to take avoiding action.

Feedback on performance should be so frequent that the formal appraisal process carries no surprises to either side. Frequent feedback can also be constructive. You can spot problems and deal with them early, so that the problem does not become a crisis and the crisis does not become a drama. The art of feedback is covered in section 19.

3. Spot the dip versus the doom loop

Fortunately, it is fairly easy to spot a dip in performance versus a genuine low performer from the way they react to missing deadlines and goals, as below:

High performer's dip	Low performer's doom loop
Recognizes the problem	Denies the problem
Accepts responsibility	Spreads the blame
Finds solutions	Finds excuses
Stays visible	Hides
Proactively works on next steps	Reactively half-delivers on next steps

With the high performer, it is worth finding out what has caused the dip in performance. It could be personal problems such as bereavement, illness or mental illness. Or it could be events conspired against the individual: the project was not set up right, or a third party dropped a commitment. These are temporary blips where you can help your team member recover personally and professionally.

The low performer will volunteer a whole host of similar excuses, but the excuses will be used to justify continued low performance. The difference is that the high performer will accept responsibility, work on the solution and will not keep on coming back with more excuses.

When in difficulty, get help

If you find yourself in a performance dip, then make sure you follow the right pattern of behaviour (above). In addition, you need to do two more things: get help and control the narrative.

Get help. When in difficulty, get help. You are at your most vulnerable. You need both personal and professional support to give comfort and to give practical advice. An objective perspective will help you see where you are and the way out of your predicament.

Control the narrative. If you listen to the company grapevine, the gossip tends to come to very simple conclusions about people. If a colleague is struggling, that will be noticed and inevitably the grapevine will want to know why. If you do not provide the narrative, the grapevine will invent a narrative, which is unlikely to help you. Bosses will do the same thing: they will make assumptions about what is going wrong. Those assumptions can be lethal to your career. Make sure you promote a positive narrative about your performance. Sell yourself and your work.

21

Dealing with difficult people

The challenge

You do not choose the colleagues you work with. Some are a joy to work with, but a few will be challenging. You have to make the most of it.

Difficult people come in two and a half flavours:

1. *Aggressive colleagues* for whom every conversation is a contest. They must win and you must lose. Some of them could start an argument in an empty room. If you let them have their way, they will trample all over you and they will enjoy it.
2. *Passive victims.* They are martyrs to the world, always suffering from misfortune and mistreatment. They want your sympathy and support. Some suffer in noble silence; a few like to whinge and whine non-stop; a few become professional victims who turn aggressive with their victimhood.
3. *People who are being difficult.* Even reasonable people need to be unreasonable at times to protect their interests or sort out a crisis. They are not problem people; they are people with a problem. These colleagues are not difficult to deal with, although it may be difficult to deal with their problem. The leadership arts of listening, coaching, the persuasive conversation and effective problem solving are enough to deal with people who are being difficult.

> **Even reasonable people need to be unreasonable at times**

The leadership challenge is to deal with people who are always difficult, not temporarily difficult. This section focuses on dealing with aggressive and passive colleagues.

The solution

Passive and aggressive colleagues enjoy it when you play their game.

Aggressive colleagues have a lifetime's experience of fighting battles and know how to win them. Fighting them is dangerous because you probably have less experience of the many devious ways they can use to make you look bad. If you fight them, be sure you can win. You will know you can win if you have all the power on your side: either you have formal power yourself or you have the informal power of strong allies. Most bullies avoid a fight which they might lose and will back off very fast when they see where the power lies.

Passive people want to be indulged in their victimhood. This is a challenge because as a leader you should have empathy with good colleagues who are going through some tough times. Help others in need as you would hope to be helped when you need it. But when victimhood becomes a state of mind, you do not help by empathizing and reinforcing that state of mind. You are a leader, not a psychotherapist. You cannot sort out their mental issues, although you can direct them to suitable support if that is required.

If the first part of the solution is to avoid playing the game that the difficult people want you to play, what is the game you should play? The simplistic answer is that you should play the leadership game. As a leader, you should not be passive and you do not need to be aggressive (although psychopaths show that this can be a successful strategy if you become skilled at it).

The middle way between being passive and aggressive is assertiveness. As an assertive leader you will respect others, but you will protect your interests when you need to. Focus on the issue, not on the personality; use reason not emotion. The different approaches are laid out in the table below:

	Passive colleagues	*Aggressive colleagues*	*Assertive leadership*
Locus of control	No control in a cruel and unfair world	Control others	Control self
Work relationships	Serve others. Not supported by others.	Win/lose: always need to win	Partnership, respectful
Adult/child relationship	Child	Adult surrounded by children	Adult to adult
Feelings	Anxious, ignored	Superior	Confident
How colleagues see them	Pity or contempt Harmless or useless	Threatening, dangerous and aggressive	Partner and colleague
Outcomes	Lose at own expense	Win at others' expense	Create a win/win

The table shows that passive and aggressive people trade in emotions. Aggressive types will happily try to force a negative emotional reaction from you by belittling you; 'that is a really dumb idea, who screwed that up, can't you do anything right?' Ignore their provocations completely. Stay calm and professional.

The best response is to force your aggressive colleague to be clear about what outcome they want to achieve and how they want to achieve it. This will drive them **Focus on the issue, not on the personality** crazy, and they will double down on the provocations. Respond by staying focused: ask them to be clear about what outcome they want from the conversation. Force them to find solutions to move to action. They may find this threatening, because solutions and actions leave them vulnerable to being the dumb person who screws up.

You have to be assertive in dealing with aggressive colleagues: if you are passive they will take advantage. If you fight aggression with aggression you play their game and you will lose. Being assertive means being clear about your interests, knowing what practical outcome you want to achieve and then keeping the conversation focused on solutions and actions. You will then be fighting on your terms, not theirs. You will be acting like a leader.

22

Lead your boss

The challenge

Everyone has a boss. Even the CEO has a boss: the chair and board of the firm. Bosses are a problem:

- They do not come with a user manual, and you cannot replace them or get your money back
- There is no training on how to deal with them
- They have power over you; you do not have power over them

You can turn these problems into a wonderful opportunity. If you can learn to manage your boss, you can manage anyone. You will also learn the twenty-first century skills of leading without formal power.

If you can manage your boss, you can manage anyone

The solution

In this section you will discover:

- What your boss really wants from you
- How to mess up with your boss
- How to adapt to your boss

What your boss really wants from you

In my research on leadership I ask bosses what they want from their teams. The results are consistent, and only partly reflect what you will see in a typical HR evaluation system. If you fulfil the following five criteria, you will be well on the way to success with your boss:

- *Proactivity.* Bosses want team members who take initiative, anticipate events, react to problems and do not need to be told what to do every five minutes. Your boss relies on you to make things happen. So make them happen.
- *Intelligence.* Bosses do not expect you to be Einstein. But they want team members who will work through problems and unexpected challenges themselves. They do not want to hold your hand, and they do not want all your problems landing back on their desk. They greatly appreciate team members who come up with new ideas.
- *Hard work.* Your boss is under pressure and needs your help in carrying the load. If you do not carry your weight, either your boss or your colleagues have to take up the slack. That is bad for morale and bad for your career. Even with remote working, it is fairly obvious who is putting in the effort and who is not. Bosses are particularly grateful to any team member who puts in discretionary effort. If you go above and beyond the call of duty by helping out on a new project or taking on an extra responsibility, that gets noticed.
- *Reliability.* This is all about doing as you say. Professionals are often diligent about what they do, but careless about what they say. Be careful to set expectations very clearly with your boss. Don't say you will 'try to' or 'hope to' do something. That will be taken as a commitment that you will do it. Either say you will do it or you will not. If success is conditional, be very clear about what those conditions are.
- *Ambition.* At first, this was a surprise factor in the list: don't ambitious team members want to replace their boss? In practice, bosses want team members who are ambitious for the firm and for the team, not just for themselves. An ambitious team member will always push harder: they will volunteer to help out and take on extra responsibility; they will come up with ideas and find ways of improving things; they will step up at moments of crisis instead of stepping back; they will find ways round the toughest challenges.

These five criteria at first seem to be very low hurdles for you to jump. But it turns out that bosses rate barely half of their team members as meeting these expectations. Show that you are proactive, intelligent, hardworking, reliable and ambitious and you will stand out from your peers.

How to mess up with your boss

I have asked thousands of leaders what they want from their team members. They have also told me, with great emotion, what really annoys them. Here are four guaranteed ways for you to mess up with your boss:

- *Disloyalty.* Many sins are forgivable, but disloyalty is not one of them. Your boss has to be able to trust you, and disloyalty breaks all the bonds of trust that your relationship depends on. Disloyalty is not just about trying to stab your boss in the back. It can be as simple as failing to stand up for your boss at a tricky moment in a meeting, or badmouthing your boss to the wrong people at the water cooler.
- *Dishonesty* is another good way to destroy trust with your boss. Dishonesty is not about bare-faced lying. It can be failing to tell the truth about what is going on and hiding problems. Stay ahead of bad news, so that it does not reach your boss before you do. Avoid surprises and control the narrative: if there is bad news, make sure you also offer some solutions as well.
- *Surprises* are a real problem for the boss. If the boss is surprised in front of other people, it shows that the boss does not know what is happening and is not in control. They lose face and lose credibility fast with surprises, which are rarely good news.
- *Excuses* are a red flag to a boss. They show that the team member is not taking responsibility and is not dealing with the problem. Most bosses are forgiving of mistakes, because **Bosses want action, not excuses** they have made mistakes themselves. But they do not want you to come to them with excuses. They want you to come to them with a clear explanation of the problem and of your proposed solution. Bosses want action, not excuses.

How to adapt to your boss

Personality and style clashes are the most frequent cause of conflict between boss and team member. If there is a clash of styles, that is a problem for you and not for the boss. Your boss will not change style for you; you have to adapt to your boss. Consultants often try to deal with style clashes by doing personality tests, such as MB/TI (Myers Briggs Type Indicators) which put people into neat little boxes. No one should be put in a box until they are dead. These tests are useful for discussion at an offsite event, but you need something more immediate to help you adapt in real time.

Your first step is to understand how you differ from your boss. Below is a list of some of the most common style differences:

- Morning versus afternoon
- Big ideas versus detail
- People focus versus task focus
- Inductive versus deductive thinking
- Numbers versus words
- Risk taking versus risk avoiding
- Controlling versus empowering
- Email versus face to face

None of these are right or wrong. But if your boss likes detail, numbers, close control and is best face to face in the morning then do not leave it until late afternoon to email your boss with a grand new, risky idea which you have sketched out in a note with no numbers. The idea may be brilliant, but it will fall on stony ground. **Adapt to the style of your boss**

Your second step is simple: adapt to the style of your boss. This is great training for dealing with clients, external stakeholders, colleagues in other departments and top management. Learn to identify their preferred working style and adapt to it: difficult working relationships will miraculously become far easier. Your payoff is that once you are the big boss, everyone will adapt to your style.

23

Become the leader people want to follow

The challenge

Life was easier for leaders in the past. Leaders had more coercive power and followers had less choice. In the days of the one company town, followers were completely dependent on one firm not just for their job, but also for their house, health and children's education. Even in the twentieth century, bosses or HR chose their teams: followers had little control over their destiny. Leaders did not need to worry about whether followers wanted to follow them or not: followers did as they were told.

Now, life is harder for leaders. Followers have higher expectations of what work should look like and what the boss should be like. They have choices: if they do not like the boss or the work, they are likely to move to a better job and better boss. In the war for talent, power is moving from employer to employee: the best staff have choices, and do you really want to have a team of mediocre staff?

Be the leader people want to follow

If you want a high-performing team, you have to be the leader people want to follow, not the leader people have to follow because of the assignment system. In the war for talent, as with all wars, life is better if you are on the winning side.

This challenge has two solutions: the basic solution and the golden solution.

The basic solution

First the good news: no leader gets ticks in all the boxes. Your followers do not expect you to be perfect, and you cannot be perfect anyway.

In my research on leadership, I have asked thousands of followers what they expect of their leaders. Here are their top five expectations:

1. *Vision.* Followers want to know where they are going, and that their future is going to be better than their past. As a leader, you are a peddler of hope, clarity and certainty especially at moments of crisis, doubt and despair. Your vision is about how you will take people where they would not have got by themselves: it goes to the heart of leadership. Fortunately, your vision does not need to be a grandiose 'change the world' vision. It is a simple story about how you will get from here to a place which is better not just for the firm and yourself, but for your team member as well. (Vision is covered in chapter 32 on 'Take Control'.)

2. *Be motivational.* 67 per cent of bosses rate themselves as good at motivation, only 32 per cent of followers agree. This is your chance to stand out from your peers. (Motivation is covered in detail in chapters 26 and 27.) For now, it is enough to note that a good vision is by itself highly motivational because it gives the team hope, clarity and purpose. You can make your vision even more motivational by telling each team member how their role is vital in helping you reach the Promised Land.

3. *Decisiveness.* Followers crave clarity and certainty. Doubt and ambiguity is toxic: it leads to anxiety, stress and excess work as your team try to anticipate your needs and react to your changing decisions. If you have a clear vision, it becomes far easier to make difficult decisions because you will know your priorities and know where you want to get to.

4. *Good in a crisis.* Crises are moments of truth, which will define you. You can be positive, proactive and supportive for 99 per cent of the time, but that will not matter if you become negative, passive and blaming in a crisis. You will be remembered for how you were for that 1 per cent of the time in a crisis.

5. *Honesty.* For followers, honesty is about trust. They need to be able to trust you to say the right thing and do the right thing. They need to trust you to look after their interests. They accept that sometimes there may be difficult conversations about expectations and performance. They prefer to have the clarity and certainty those conversations create than to live with doubt and anxiety.

Leadership honesty is not 'weak form' politician's honesty where you are honest until a court has found you guilty of lying. It is 'strong form' honesty where you face the brutal truth and deal with it openly and constructively.

These may not seem to be demanding expectations, but less than half of leaders are rated well on these attributes by their teams. Meet these expectations and you will be in danger of becoming the leader people want to follow.

The golden solution

After analysing all the replies from followers about their leaders, one question turned out to be a very good predictor of whether a leader would be seen as being good on the top five qualities of a leader: vision, being motivational, decisiveness, good in a crisis and honesty. It is the golden question which will make you the leader people want to follow, not have to follow.

Here is the golden question for leaders:

'My boss cares for me and my career' (agree/disagree on a five-point scale)

This is so simple and so obvious. We rate the performance of our boss based on how they treat us. Perceptions may be false, but consequences of perceptions are real. The way they rate you determines whether they want to work for you. So it pays to show that you care for each team member and their career.

Showing you care is the golden key Show you care and they will see you through rose-tinted glasses: they will interpret all your foibles and your performance positively. Conversely, we have all had to work for bosses who clearly have no interest in us at all. It is a demotivating experience and you probably have a fairly negative view of how that boss performed.

Caring does not mean courting popularity and having a bowl of candy by your desk. It means:

- Understanding the career aspirations of each follower: find the right projects, experiences, training and support to help them.

- Giving frequent and constructive feedback on performance so that they can improve. Have difficult conversations early and positively, if necessary.
- Respecting their personal lives and work life balance: do not issue urgent and important work requirements every Friday evening.

It is hard to care for each team member if you have dozens of team members or direct reports. You may fool yourself into thinking that 30 minutes once a fortnight is enough time with each team member if it is quality time. You need to invest enough time, not just quality time, in relationships which matter to you professionally and personally.

Showing you care for each team member is the golden key to being rated as a good boss by your team.

24

Become the trusted colleague

The challenge

In the past, managers made things happen through people they controlled. Now you have to make things happen through people you do not control. You rely on other departments, and maybe external suppliers and even customers, for your success. Even your own team does not want to be controlled. Lack of control changes everything for a manager. You can no longer rely on your formal authority and budget for success. You need informal power which stretches far beyond your immediate span of control.

In the twenty-first century, you need a network of willing allies if you are to succeed. This is tough because the allies you want will all have their own, different, priorities which may clash or compete with your priorities. You can argue your case and you may win your battles. But when you win a battle, you lose a potential ally. You have to keep working with the people you compete with: you need allies, not enemies.

It is better to win a friend than to win a battle

The challenge is to move beyond a series of transactional battles which you win or lose to get your way. You need to build trusted relationships where you can work with colleagues and find win/win solutions not win/lose battles. Often, it is better to win a friend than to win a battle. It is far easier to resolve differences with people you trust than to fight battles with colleagues where there is no trust.

This chapter is about how you can become influential in your organization by becoming the trusted colleague.

The solution

To succeed, you need to be trusted by your boss, your team and your colleagues. Trust is the currency of informal power and influence in any organization. If you are not trusted, you cannot succeed.

The one way you cannot build trust is by saying 'trust me', unless you want to sound like a second-hand car salesman or a politician. Trust is a small word with a big meaning. Here is an equation, with all its spurious mathematical accuracy, to help you break trust down into a few actionable items:

$$t = \frac{s \times g \times c}{r}.$$

Where:

- t = trust
- s = social alignment
- g = goal alignment
- c = credibility
- r = risk

We will look at each element and show how you can use it to become the trusted and influential colleague and partner within and beyond your organization.

1. Social alignment

When you notice two business people meeting for the first time, they often start by chatting about apparently nothing very much. This is not a waste of time. They are normally finding out whether they have anything in common with each other: professional background, interests, families, places lived, events attended and so on. There is a reason for this. We find it far easier to trust people who are like ourselves. That is bad for diversity, but good for efficiency: it is easier for us to read and understand people who think like us.

Societies with high social alignment have high trust, and have the lowest need for personal security and lawyers. Societies with much greater social diversity have more need for legal protection (lawyers) and personal protection (guns). Japan versus the United States, for instance.

You can build personal alignment even if you are working from home. Curate your Zoom background to disclose what you want to about your personal life: some books, objects or photos that others will notice. This gives you the chance to start a personal conversation. When you disclose something about yourself, the other person will want to reciprocate. As you discover more about each other, you will find some points of common interest and the process of social alignment will have started.

2. Goal alignment

It is very hard to trust someone who has competing goals to yours. If they are in it for themselves, then you are likely to have a battle, not an alliance. This is where you need some creativity to find the common goal. At its most basic level within the firm, you are both working to make the firm more profitable. In practice, that is asking colleagues to act altruistically which is a big ask. You have to show that what you are doing is consistent with what they are doing. For instance, you have to show that your idea is consistent with the rules and needs of finance, HR, IT and all the other departments you work with. If your idea breaks their rules and their budgets, expect a battle.

Dealing with external stakeholders should be easier: if you are talking to each other, both of you already hope to gain something from the conversation. All you are doing is defining the mutual win/win. But even here you may need some creativity. If you are selling, the immediate buyer may well enter into a price negotiation. Your challenge is to show that there is a bigger win than immediate price: maybe lifetime cost, ease of use, your product may reduce other costs or improve your client's customer retention. If you negotiate on price you have a win/lose battle. If you find the bigger goal, you can have a win/win discussion.

3. Credibility

Lost credibility is like a broken vase: you can, with difficulty, repair it but it will never really be the same again. Ultimately, credibility is about doing as you say. Most professionals will be insulted if you suggest that they do not do as they say. They will

Lost credibility is like a broken vase

be half-right to be insulted, because professionals always strive to deliver on their promises. The reason that they are only half-right is that the problem is not in the doing: it is in the saying.

Professionals do not like to disappoint. When asked to do something, you may well reply that you will 'do your best', 'see what is possible' or 'look into it'. What you say and what is heard is completely different. You know you are not saying that it will be done: you will use best efforts. What is heard is a concrete commitment to making it happen.

Now roll the camera forward and see what happens in this movie of tragedy and drama. Two weeks later you come back and honestly report that you looked into it, did your best and found that it was not possible. You have gone out of your way to fulfil your side of the bargain. And all your credibility has been lost, because the other person thought that you had promised to do it. At this stage, you can enter the classic 'he said, you said, they didn't, etc.' discussion. That simply serves to make both aggrieved parties even more aggrieved.

The solution is to have a difficult conversation about expectations at the start, not an impossible conversation about outcomes at the end. Before you take on any commitment, with your boss or team or colleagues, be crystal clear about what you will or will not do. If success is conditional, make sure those conditions are understood unambiguously. Then make sure you are set up for success before you start.

4. Risk

Risk is analogue, not digital. The more the risk, the more trust is needed. I may trust a stranger in the street to tell me the way to the post office; I would be unwise to trust a stranger in the street with my life savings.

Risk is analogue, not digital

You have three ways of dealing with risky situations where you need the trust and support of colleagues:

- Reduce the risk
- Borrow some trust
- Increase the risk

Reduce the risk

This is the obvious solution for any risky proposal. You can probably find ways to phase the programme, or perhaps do some more research to test the idea, or do a test market or share the investment with partners, or buy insurance. If you can do this, do it. But sometimes, you cannot de-risk a project very much. Building a next generation microchip plant costs billions and half a chip plant is useless: you have to go all in or not at all.

Borrow some trust

For a risky proposal, find a credible sponsor to support you. The proposal will then rest on the credibility of your sponsor, not just your credibility. You can see this in consumer advertising: if the sports shoes, tennis racket or golf clubs are good enough for the world champion who endorses them, they must be good enough for me. The credibility of the champion provides a simple way of choosing between the endless brands and models available on the market.

Increase the risk

All risk is relative. There is a risk of doing something and there is a risk of doing nothing. This is classically used by CEOs who like to create a 'burning platform' to push their change agenda. Their unsubtle pitch is this: 'make this slightly painful change now because the cost of not changing is far greater pain later'. You can use the same approach: 'if we do this we invest/ risk $1 million; if we don't invest then we will lose $2 million per year in reduced market share etc'. Use risk for your advantage.

PART FOUR

LEADING TEAMS

25

Select the right team

The challenge

Selecting the right team goes right to the heart of your IPM agenda (see chapter 32) as a leader: Idea, People, and Money and Machine. The right people will climb mountains for you, the wrong people will make mountains out of molehills and will not even climb those.

You face three challenges in finding the right team:

1. Finding the skills
Despite the war for talent, there is no shortage of people with the right skills and experience. The cost of specialized talent, such as legal or IT, can be very high. But if you pay the price you can find the talent. Most firms have reasonably good HR processes which will enable you to identify and select the right skills, so you can rely on that to help you. All too often references are not checked, with fatal consequences. Never skip references.

2. Attracting the skills
If you want to attract the A* team, not the B team, you have to be the leader people want to work for, not the leader they have to work for. The recruitment process is not a one-way street. You have to sell yourself and your firm to the candidate. Becoming the leader people want to follow was covered in chapter 23.

Becoming the firm recruits want to join may not be entirely in your hands. The more attractive the organization, the harder the selection process is: joining the Marines, or a major investment bank or professional services firm is gruelling for graduates. The challenge of the process is part of the allure: it is an early chance for graduates to prove themselves and to join like-minded over-achievers. However attractive your organization may, or may not be, you still have to sell yourself. The chances are that recruits will be looking at several similar organizations to yours, and much of the difference will come down to who they meet and who they think they will work for. You are a vital part of the product, so make sure you are an asset and not a liability.

3. Finding the right values

People are hired for their skills and fired for their values. Think of all the

People are hired for their skills and fired for their values

most dysfunctional colleagues you have worked with. The chances are that they did not lack the skills for their job. Instead, they had the wrong values for the job.

The solution

For the most part, the solution is simple: use the established HR processes of the firm. If they already work, don't reinvent the wheel. The one area where many recruiting systems fail is around values. This matters because you can train skills, but you cannot train values. A person with great skills but poor values is toxic. A person with strong values but weak skills can learn.

As an employer you can be neutral about styles, but you cannot be neutral about values. A range of styles can be useful for a team: extrovert and introvert, task focus and people focus, inductive and deductive thinkers. There is no right and wrong style. But on values you need to be judgemental. Some values are universal needs, such as honesty and hard work. Others may be more specific to your firm such as optimism and adaptability. Be clear about the values that are non-negotiable for your firm, and recruit to them.

Two examples will make the point and show how you can recruit to values.

MetLife

MetLife found that it was recruiting and losing thousands of agents per year at great cost. They needed to find a better way of recruiting. As a test, they screened for optimism which they thought might be a core value for successful sales people. Then they recruited all the people who just failed the skills test but scored highly on optimism. The results were astonishing. The low skills/high optimism candidates quickly picked up the skills and outsold their higher skilled colleagues by more than 50 per cent, with a much lower dropout rate. The experiment has become policy and has been repeated in many other sales roles in other industries such as real estate.

Timpson's

Timpson's runs a chain of shoe repair shops, which are micro-businesses staffed by one or two people. They used to recruit to skills, but found that skilled cobblers were rarely good at dealing with staff or business. So they switched to recruiting to values: in their words, they recruit entirely by personality. After an interview and a trial day, each candidate is placed against a grid which has a series of cartoon characters.
The positive ones include: Mr Happy, Miss Cheerful, Mr Helpful. Negative characters include: Mr Lazy, Miss Grumpy, Mr Fib.

Recruit to values, not just to skills

Candidates with the right character succeed, those with the wrong character fail. This radical approach means that they are even able to recruit ex-offenders, which supports their rehabilitation. With the right values, anyone can succeed.

Ultimately the solution is very simple. Recruit to values, not just to skills.

26

Create a motivated team

The challenge

There is an epidemic of alienation at work. A recent Gallup poll reported that only 15 per cent of employees feel engaged at work globally. Low engagement is a recipe for low performance.

The problem of low engagement is surprising because there is an entire industry of motivation gurus, wellbeing gurus, academic insight, psychological theory and consulting support which should have made alienation a thing of the past. But it is still with us.

If the solution is not working, it is often because we are asking the wrong question. Although the experts are very clear about their solution, they are not always clear about what problem they are solving. The problem which most solutions imply is this: 'how can we motivate employees?'

You cannot tell people to be motivated

This is fundamentally the wrong question to ask. It makes two assumptions:

- *Staff are naturally demotivated.* Alienated workers might have been the natural state of affairs in the Industrial Revolution when unskilled workers toiled for 12 hours a day in gruesome conditions. But most professionals today are highly skilled and have a high sense of intrinsic motivation: they have pride in their work and want to do well.
- *Motivation is something that you do to people.* This is also a false assumption. You cannot tell people to be motivated, happy or positive. These things come from within. If your motivation

depends on someone else, you let yourself become a victim of fate and circumstance. You can demotivate people, but motivating them is far harder.

It is time to reframe the motivation challenge. By assuming that professionals are intrinsically motivated and that motivation comes from within, we find that there are two challenges for leaders:

- How do you create the conditions in which your team will rediscover their intrinsic motivation? That is the focus of this section.
- How do you avoid demotivating your team? We will explore this in the next chapter.

The solution (in theory)

Given that there is an entire industry devoted to motivation, it is worth knowing the theories which are behind the industry. Two main theories stand out: Maslow's hierarchy of needs and McGregor's theory X and Y. We will explore each and see how you can use them as a leader.

Maslow's hierarchy of needs

Maslow's core insight is that we are all needs junkies. As soon as we have met one need, we discover another need. We live on a hedonic treadmill: no matter how fast we run to meet our needs we always find we have to run even harder to meet our ever-growing needs. Maslow captured this in the form of a pyramid. You start at the bottom: if you have no food or water, then that is all you care about. Slowly, you work up the hierarchy of needs until you become a billionaire and you worry about whether you can achieve immortality by having a university established in your name.

Our needs change over time. If we lose our job, then suddenly we will no longer be focused on our esteem (level 2), we will be very focused on getting a job and the safety of an income (level 4)

Below is Maslow's hierarchy of needs. See where you fit in.

1. Self-actualization: become the most of who you are
2. Esteem: respect, status, self-esteem, recognition, freedom
3. Love and belonging: friendship, love, intimacy and a sense of connection

4. Safety needs: personal security, health, employment, property
5. Physiological needs: food, water, shelter, clothing

From the management perspective, this has some limited use. The problem is knowing what stage your colleagues are at, and what you are meant to do about it. You probably should not start asking colleagues if they are at the love stage: your enquiry could be misinterpreted. In practice, most people in settled jobs are at the esteem stage. They want status, recognition and self-esteem from doing a worthwhile job and freedom in the form of high autonomy. If that is all you take from Maslow's hierarchy of needs, you will have a good formula for supporting your team positively.

McGregor's Theory X and Y

What do you think of your colleagues? Do you believe that they are inherently idle, that they will do the minimum needed to get by, they avoid responsibility and act only in their self-interest? If you believe this, you are a supporter of Theory X and you will motivate your team by explicit rewards and punishments. You will supervise them closely and expect them to do exactly as they are told. This was how managers worked in the Industrial Revolution. Arguably, it is how algorithms manage delivery people and warehouse workers today. Theory X works best where work is standardized, routine and predictable.

You may have a better view of your colleagues. Perhaps you believe that they are intrinsically motivated to do a good job; they will take on responsibility and do not need their boss supervising them closely all day. If you believe this, you are likely to subscribe to Theory Y, which is more suited to the world of professional work. Theory Y works well where work is varied, ambiguous and needs some level of creativity and insight, which is a good approximation of the world of professional work.

Pay is often a demotivational tool

Theory X still pervades the world of motivation. Plenty of firms still use carrots and sticks to motivate: pay is seen as a vital motivational tool. In practice, pay is often a demotivational tool. If you get the raise or bonus you expected, that is not motivational. But if you get less than you expected, or less than a colleague, that can be very demotivational. And even if you get more than you expected, the hedonic treadmill just starts moving faster than ever: your expectations will rise and you will move on to your next set of needs and wants.

A soft form of theory X is when firms resort to putting slides and table tennis tables in the office, offering in-house therapy and all-you-can-drink smoothies. This may be fashionable, but it still adopts the nineteenth-century approach of using extrinsic rewards to motivate staff.

Firms struggle with theory Y. Fortunately, pioneering work with education systems around the world is showing how you can put theory Y into practice by creating system-wide conditions in which professionals rediscover their intrinsic motivation. That is the focus of the next part of the solution.

The solution (in practice)

The practical solution shifts focus. It looks at how you can create the conditions where everyone in your system, firm or team can rediscover their intrinsic motivation. This helps you as a leader because:

a. You do not need to be personally inspirational or motivational to have a motivated team
b. You do not need a PhD in psychology to work out the needs and profile of each team member
c. Responsibility for motivation shifts from you to the team member: you cannot and should not tell them to be happy, motivated or positive
d. As a leader there are practical things you can do to create the conditions where your whole team can rediscover their intrinsic motivation

There are four things you need to put in place to build the motivation of your team: supportive relationships, autonomy, mastery and purpose. These four factors can be summarized as RAMP:

- **Relationships** which are supportive
- **Autonomy**
- **Mastery**
- **Purpose**

We encountered RAMP before (chapter 4) as the formula for making sure that you find the context where you will flourish. As a leader, you can use the same formula to create the conditions where your team will flourish. We will look at each part of the RAMP formula in turn.

Relationships which are supportive

If you are being undermined by your boss and your colleagues, you will struggle. The traditional view of management was command and control, and was not very supportive of staff. Highly skilled and motivated staff do not need micro-management. They need the right sort of support to succeed. Being supportive is not about trying to be popular: it is about earning respect and trust. You can do this by:

- making sure that you delegate interesting work
- ensuring your team has the tools and resources to do the job
- coaching your team to find solutions to problems and to grow their skills
- protecting your team from political interference
- understanding and supporting their career ambitions, including having difficult but constructive conversations about performance when necessary
- respecting the personal needs of your team

Supportive relationships extend beyond your relationship with your team.

Being supportive is not about trying to be popular

It is also about how your team does or does not support each other. Foster collaborative, not competitive, relationships across your team if you need them to work as a team.

Autonomy

Professionals do not like being bossed around. They crave autonomy. This is very good news. It means that the best way to manage professionals is to manage them less. Do not micro-manage them. Delegate meaningful work to them and trust them to deliver. Most professionals are likely to over-deliver, not under-deliver. Let their professional pride drive them to perform instead of traditional performance management and control. How you can delegate well is covered in chapter 30.

Mastery

If you lack the skills for today's role and you are not growing the skills you need for tomorrow's role, you are unlikely to feel motivated. You have a vital role as a leader in helping your team on their mastery journey. The two most important things you can do are:

- Delegate the right work, which should be stretching so that they learn, but the work should not be unachievable.
- Creating a learning culture. Encouraging your team to debrief regularly and learn from each other not only helps mastery, but is also a good way of building supportive and positive relationships across the team.

Purpose

A McKinsey survey in 2021 showed that work is an important part of people's sense of purpose for over 70 per cent of staff: the more senior you become, the more work becomes a source of purpose in life. This is not surprising, because work is such a large part of life. It gives your staff structure and meaning to the rhythms of life, and it gives a sense of community and belonging. For more senior staff, it is also a source of pride and prestige.

The move to hybrid work led to people re-examining their connection with the world of work and to the 'Great Resignation' over 2021–22 when record numbers of staff decided to re-order their priorities and purpose, having discovered the joys of working from home.

Ultimately, a sense of purpose is deeply personal. You cannot tell people what their purpose is, but you can nudge them to discover their sense of purpose. Here are some things which will help people discover a strong sense of purpose:

a. Work for an organization which has a real sense of purpose. Obvious examples include the armed forces, religious organizations and charities where talented people trade wealth and comfort for a deep sense of purpose. For profit organizations can also offer purpose in the form of:

- change the world: tech companies
- save the world: health firms
- improve the world: consulting firms

- serve the world: banks, outsourcing firms
- give people what they need or want: consumer goods and services

b. Reinforce a sense of community and belonging. Work is not purely transactional: it is also about positive and supportive relationships. A workplace which fosters supportive relationships can drive a sense of purpose by creating the community and belonging which Maslow identified as being a fundamental human need.

c. Create flexible work structures so that your team can balance their personal sense of purpose (family, outside interests) with their professional work.

d. Foster mastery which is a powerful driver of purpose in its own right as many an artist or potter will attest. Becoming recognised as an expert or leader in your area of expertise sustains both purpose and motivation.

27

Be a motivational team leader

The challenge

Being motivational is one of the top five expectations that followers have of their leaders. The good news is that 67 per cent of leaders think that they are good at motivation. The bad news is that only 32 per cent of followers think that their bosses are any good at motivation. There is a yawning motivation gap between reality and perception.

Asking leaders to be motivational is to ask the wrong question. It is not the job of the leader to inspire the team each day, perhaps by standing on the desk and making a rousing speech. If team members are not intrinsically motivated to perform, then either the conditions at work are wrong or you have the wrong team. That means you either need to change work conditions, or you need to change the team. Ultimately, motivation comes from within. Any team member who relies on their manager to generate their own motivation is probably not the right team member.

Ultimately, motivation comes from within

With the right conditions in place, the right team will be intrinsically motivated to perform. That means your job is not to inspire and motivate them. Your job is to avoid demotivating them. The fact that only 32 per cent of followers think that bosses are any good at motivation, suggests that a majority of managers may be actively, if accidentally, demotivating their teams.

All of this is good news for leaders. You do not need to add to your job requirements the demands of being inspirational and motivational. Most leaders are human beings and would struggle with such requirements. To be motivational all you need to do is:

a. Create the conditions in which your team will rediscover their intrinsic motivation (see the previous chapter, 26).

b. Avoid demotivating your team, by accident or by design: that is the focus of this chapter.

The solution

Demotivating your team is very easy to do accidentally. Some leaders make an art form of it. We should be grateful to such leaders, because we can learn from them how to avoid messing up, and by

Demotivating your team is very easy to do accidentally

inference we can learn what we should do. It is always easier to learn from setbacks than from successes. So I am forever indebted to the worst manager I ever had to endure: David X was the walking textbook on how to demotivate anyone.

Here is David X's recipe for demotivation, and how you can learn from it:

1. Be unclear about goals and deadlines, and then change your mind. Create maximum uncertainty and confusion. Always bring deadlines forwards to create as much stress as possible. Lesson: be clear and consistent in your decision making.

2. Delegate routine rubbish only, unless a project has gone wrong in which case delegate that and all the blame which goes with it. Lesson: stretch and develop your team by delegating stretching but achievable tasks (as well as inevitable routine tasks).

3. Keep control of the photocopy machine key. Show you do not trust your team and make sure they do not have the resources to succeed. Lesson: learn to trust your team and set them up to succeed, not fail.

4. Spread your gloom and pessimism to the whole team. Lesson: leaders are peddlers of hope, certainty and clarity. If you are not positive, no one else will be positive for you. Teams pick up their values and mood from their leader. If you wonder why your team is nasty and miserable, look in the mirror. If they are positive, energetic and constructive, pat yourself on the back.

5. Coach your team by criticizing them frequently in public. Lesson: criticism does not work and is not necessary: find the solution, not the problem with your team.

6. Don't support your team at moments of truth in public. Let them fight for themselves: survival of the fittest. Lesson: loyalty is a two-way street. Just as bosses expect followers to support them loyally at moments of truth, so followers expect the same from their bosses.

7. Never praise anyone because that is a sign of weakness. Lesson: people like recognition. Spread your praise: don't have favourites and an 'in' team and 'out' team.

8. Expect your team to laugh at your feeble, sexist jokes and to praise your great ideas. Require them to admire your trophy house and spouse and their very special holidays. Lesson: grow up.

9. Don't allow dissent and crush any new ideas unless they are good, (in which case steal them), because the only person who is allowed to have good ideas is the boss. Lesson: the best ideas come from the group, not an individual. Listen to your team: hear their ideas and encourage constructive dissent.

10. Make any feedback an unpleasant surprise at the year-end review. Lesson: continual and constructive feedback helps your team.

11. Get angry and rule by fear, especially if you are having a bad day. Lesson: learn to wear the mask of leadership: positive, practical and action focused.

12. Show you don't care for your team or their futures. Don't listen to their needs, hopes and fears because that is their problem, not yours. Lesson: if you want to be the boss that people want to work for, show you care for your team. See the golden rule in chapter 23.

Loyalty is a two-way street

The real lesson from all this is that you do not need to be a motivational manager. Most team members are intrinsically motivated to do a good job. Don't make motivation complicated.

Sometimes, all you need for a motivated team is to stop demotivating them.

28

Lead teams you cannot see

The challenge

The advent of hybrid and remote working has raised the bar for leaders. Everything is harder when you lead a remote team. That is good news. If you can learn to lead a remote team, you can lead any team. You will also set yourself apart from many of your peers.

We have discovered that the office is a very good place for very bad leaders in two ways:

- Offices are forgiving of mediocre management. In an office you can spot a mistake fast and fix it fast by walking across the room. With remote work you may not even realize you miscommunicated for two days, by which time a small problem can escalate into a major drama.
- Offices are paradise for micro-managing control freaks. In the office, managers can help (interfere) at will. Remote work forces leaders to delegate more. They have to trust that their team will do the right thing even when they cannot be seen.

Offices are forgiving of mediocre management

Over the last six years I have been working with global and remote teams to identify the main challenges they face and the solutions they have found. The three biggest challenges for leaders of remote teams are:

1. *Skills.* It is harder to execute all the basic tasks of leadership when you work remotely, because misunderstandings happen more easily and are harder to fix. For instance, the first person to

work out how to motivate people by email will make a fortune. It is a fortune which is unlikely to be made. Likewise, goal setting, problem solving, performance management, difficult conversations, influencing people and decisions are far harder when you are remote: you cannot have the ad hoc dialogue of the office which enables so many leadership tasks.

2. *Communication*. We communicate more than ever, but understand each other as little as ever. Technology has advanced faster than humanity. The leadership challenge is to tame the communications beast: communicate less, but better.

3. *Trust* is the glue that keeps teams together. Trust is much harder to build when people do not see or know each other. For established teams which went hybrid, they had a legacy of trust they could rely on. But new teams and new team members struggle to build the trust they need to work together well.

This book focuses on the skills of leadership, so this section will not attempt to summarize the rest of the book. Instead, this section will focus on the linked challenges of communications and trust. Good communication builds trust and vice versa.

The solution

Build trust across your team

Building trust is the focus of chapter 24. It is key to building power and influence far beyond the formal power of your budget and span of control. But for the special case of building trust in a hybrid or global team, there is one very simple action you can take: get the team together in a room.

Find an excuse to hold an offsite event for your team: strategy review, training day, planning meeting, as you please. The formal agenda should have value, but the real value is the informal agenda of getting your team members to know each other. Even on global teams, the consistent finding is that if you invest in the plane tickets and get people to meet in person, the effect is transformative. When your team members get to know each other through a shared experience, they build trust and that

We communicate more than ever but understand each other as little as ever

raises the quality of communication dramatically for months after the event. This is especially important where you have new or inexperienced team members.

Clearly, there is far more to becoming the trusted leader. That will be dealt with in the section on trust. In the meantime, arrange that meeting. You are even allowed to have some fun.

Tame the communications beast

A common complaint on global and hybrid teams is that you can spend all day communicating and none of the day doing things. Reducing the quantity of communication forces you and your team to raise the quality of communication: you have to make sure you get it right first time, every time. Clear communication reflects clear thinking, so forcing this discipline helps everyone.

There are two simple things you can do to tame the communications beast.

First, agree the rhythms and routines of communicating. Agree when your team will be available for Zoom calls, when they will be expected to respond to asynchronous communications (emails, texts, WhatsApp) and when they are expected to work uninterrupted. You need to create boundaries and respect them. This should be a team decision and you should stick to it as a team or change it as a team.

Second, start each day with a YTH team meeting. In this meeting each team member has 90 seconds to summarize three things for the rest of the team:

- Y: this is what I did Yesterday
- T: this is what I will do Today
- H: here is where I may need Help

Many successful global and hybrid teams use this to keep the team on track. In one short meeting, everyone on the team knows what everyone else is doing and any misunderstandings, problems or logistical **Avoid death by detail** matters can be sorted out fast. Being brief forces your team to focus on what is most important: The YTH meeting eliminates much of the noisy communication which happens throughout the day, where team members are all trying to check out what each other is doing.

The YTH meeting is also a very good leadership tool. It does four things for you:

- Reduces the communication burden: you quickly get a picture of what is happening.
- Helps you identify where to invest your time in supporting your team, because they will be asking for your help.
- Ensures your team is working on the right priorities: they will tell you what they expect to do today.
- Gives you a strong accountability tool: you can check that each team member has done yesterday what they said they would do yesterday.

There are many variations of the YTH meeting. Find a version which works for you. The point is to be much more structured, purposeful and deliberate in how you communicate remotely. If you replicate the informal and ad hoc communications of the office, you will drown in communication.

29

Build your remote or hybrid team

The challenge

In an office, the rules and values of a team may be unwritten but they are well known. Every team evolves its own code of conduct which every team member picks up by observation and by trial and error. There is no need to create a team charter, because the team knows the rules of engagement from practice.

On a remote team you suddenly need a new set of rules, and you cannot observe each other to discover what the new unwritten rules are. Answers to the simplest questions are elusive:

- What are the core working hours?
- When should we be available for virtual meetings?
- Should there be times when team members are not interrupted so that they can work?

As with all things to do with remote, hybrid and global teams you have to be much more purposeful and deliberate in everything you do. You cannot just hope that a new working pattern emerges out of the chaos. You have to work with your team to agree the new way of working. That is the focus of this chapter.

The solution

Moving to hybrid working is like starting a new team. All the old rules of how things worked in the office are no longer relevant, because you are no longer in the office all the time. This is a wonderful opportunity to re-set expectations and working patterns. Experience from the best global teams is that you can do this by holding a Methods Adoption Workshop. You can call the workshop whatever you want, but the essence of it is simple: sit down with your team (virtually, if you have to) and agree how you will work as a team. The result is a team charter which makes explicit all the implicit team rules which evolve in an office.

You will discover that obvious questions can lead to unexpected answers. One team asked: 'what should our core working hours be?' The answer was that core hours were only 10–3: no meetings or emails were expected outside those hours. That meant that some people could work straight through from 9am to 5pm. Other team members with caring responsibilities did core working hours plus 7am to 8am and 7.30pm to 9.30pm when they could work uninterrupted. The new way of working was highly flexible.

You cannot dictate the team charter: it has to come from the team so that they have a commitment to the rules. They may also improve your solutions. One firm decided to support flexible working by creating on-site nurseries. That worked very well at the factory and was a disaster at the office. At the factory, you cannot work from home so the nursery was vital. Office workers pointed out that an office-based nursery forced them to come to the office and destroyed the whole point of hybrid working. They agreed that office workers would receive an allowance for a nursery near to their homes instead.

Obvious questions can lead to unexpected answers

To make it practical, below are some of the questions you may want to explore with your team. Add, change or delete the questions as you see fit. Do what works for you and your team. After your first workshop, you will have some answers. You will then discover that not all the answers work as intended, and that you did not ask all the right questions. That is fine: this is a structured process of discovery. Run a second and third workshop which lets you replicate the informal process of discovery that happens in the office. Quickly, you will establish working patterns which work for you and your team.

Outline of a Methods Adoption Workshop

1. *Preliminaries*
   * Welcome, introductions, objectives, agenda

2. *Communications*
   * When will we be available for emails, meetings and calls? Identify core working hours and when team members can work without interruptions.
   * How will we keep each other up to date (daily YTH meeting?)
   * What technology platforms will we use?
   * Where will we work and when? How often should we be in the office, and when?
   * Meeting protocols: 60 minutes or 50? How to ensure all contribute, can we have 50/50 in/out of office meetings?

   Conduct an acid test on some of the outcomes. Is it OK to email someone at 3am in an emergency, or should we call them if it really is an emergency?

3. *Working patterns*
   * What days should we be in the office or at home? All or some of the team?
   * How will we deal with holidays, emergencies and cover?

4. *Decision making*
   This section alone can be an entire workshop. Focus on a few key decisions to start with. This section is often best done in person with a flip chart where the team can collectively map out the desired RACI (Responsible, Accountable, Consulted, Informed) by decision. Where you are running the session remotely, focus down to the bare essentials of decision making for your team.
   * What are the essential/regular decisions we have to make, and which do we want to focus on?
   * Who has decision-making rights (RACI?) for each decision?
   * Acid test the outcome: how will we deal with disagreements, etc.?

5. *Professional Development*

- How can we support new team members? (mentoring, training, networks, values etc.)
- How can we manage performance remotely?
- How can we manage workloads remotely?
- How can we support work–life balance and avoid excessive stress?

6. *Values in action*

This section is vital, but can lead to waffle. A good way in is to do a WWW/ EBI (see chapter 42) on values displayed while Working from Home (WFH): What Went Well in terms of values that enabled the team to perform remotely and what is Even Better If…. This will identify the essential values your team need to maintain going forwards. Process for this section:

- WWW and EBI on values in action currently regarding WFH/ hybrid working.
- Identify the top three values the team want to focus on in future: stay focused here.
- Acid test the core values: how will each value play out in a critical incident?

Note that on remote/global teams some values and mindsets seem to stand out:

- Professional regard, which minimizes unnecessary conflict.
- Kindness, because people need more support when they are remote.
- Growth: you need people who are willing to learn and adapt.

7. *Plumbing*

No one cares about plumbing, until it goes wrong. Then there is a crisis. Pre-empt the crisis:

- What are the minimum acceptable conditions for home working (technology, broadband, computers, tech support, workspace, desk, chair, health and safety etc.)?
- How do we support team members who do not have minimum acceptable conditions?

Pre-empt the crisis

30

Delegate well

The challenge

Delegation goes to the heart of management. First-time managers have to move from asking 'how can I do this?' to 'who can do this?' You cannot do it all yourself. You are as good as your team, so use them well.

As an exercise, ask yourself how many genuinely productive hours you can deliver in a day. When I ask groups this question, most answers are around 5–6 hours a day of really productive work. That may be an overestimate. But as a manager, you should be able to deliver 50, 500 or 5,000 hours of productive work every day. You deliver more productive hours by building a productive team. The limit to your productivity is not your time, but your team. Make sure you have the right team and delegate well to it.

At the heart of the delegation challenge is the problem of control. Managers are meant to be in control. Delegation feels like surrendering control. But managers are meant to delegate. As soon as you delegate, you weaken your level of control. You become vulnerable because you have to trust other people to perform tasks as well, or better, than you would have done them.

Have the right team and delegate well to it

It is human nature to suspect that other people are unlikely to be as good as you are. There are always excuses for not delegating:

- This is too important
- This is too urgent
- This is too difficult for the team
- It is faster for me to do it anyway

Every excuse is essentially a vote of no confidence in your team, and your team will know that. The reality is that if you dare not delegate to your team, either you have the wrong team or the team has the wrong boss.

Delegation is vital to management, and it is not done very well.

This section explores what you should delegate. Chapter 17, Set Goals, shows how you can delegate.

The solution

There are two ways of deciding what you can delegate.

The first way is to ask yourself 'what can I delegate?' If you ask this question, you are likely to come up with a very short list of answers. As you look at each important task and project, you will realize that you have to stay in control: it is not something you can realistically delegate. As a result, you will delegate only some routine rubbish and a few minor projects. You will be like most other managers who struggle to delegate well.

As a manager you have to set your team up for success

Alternatively, you can ask yourself 'what can I absolutely never delegate?' You are likely to come up with another fairly short list. There is very little that cannot reasonably be delegated. Most importantly, even if you delegate 100 per cent of your responsibilities, you can delegate zero per cent of your accountability. Whatever you delegate, you are still accountable for the outcome. Make sure you set your team up for success in whatever you delegate to them.

There are just five areas where you cannot delegate responsibility completely:

1. *Setting strategy and direction.* Leaders take people where they would not have got by themselves, so setting the direction is core to what you do. Again, you may make the final decision and you have to sell the decision to your team and colleagues, but much of the insight and grunt work can come from elsewhere.
2. *Recruiting your team.* Ultimately, you have to decide who is on your team. But often the best judges of new team members are existing team members, even if the final decision is yours. They are often vital in selling the role: people want to join a positive team.

3. *Performance management and assessments.* Although you have to do this, much of the work should be done for you. 360-degree reviews are routine and HR can run the process. Self-assessment is common: even on car production lines front-line workers monitor and manage their own performance with the support of huge amounts of data at each work station. Let people assess and performance manage themselves: they will often be more critical than you would dare to be. You can then simply approve their self-assessment.

4. *Negotiating and managing budgets.* As a manager you have to set your team up for success. That means securing the right budget and resources for their work. The team may help you make the case, but they cannot fight all of your budget battles for you. You have to step up at budget time.

5. *Running interference.* Senior management has an endless ability to make life difficult by asking for last-minute bespoke reports, changing priorities, shifting resources, demanding budget cuts and starting new initiatives. This can cause chaos for your team if you react positively to every new demand from on high. The thankless task of stopping such interference makes life far easier and more productive for your team.

If you focus only on those five priorities you can be an effective leader. But in practice there are four more things which will consume your time:

6. *Focus on one key project or priority.* You and your team will have a long list of priorities. But there is probably just one where you will make a real difference: this is your potential claim to fame. Focus your effort on that project, and delegate all the others. Even on your top project, you will be able to delegate many elements of it to your team.

7. *Coaching your team.* Delegating does not mean abandoning your team. You need to coach them when they need help. Do not let your team delegate problems back up to you. Coach them to find a solution and let them act on their solution.

8. *Dealing with noise.* Organizations are noisy. There is a huge amount of routine which adds little value, but is still important for keeping things going. Some of this can be delegated, some cannot: you

cannot delegate every email, and you cannot avoid routine meetings which you are meant to attend. It is easy to drown in noise: just responding to all the routine matters of management can be a full-time job. Keep focused on where you will make a difference: focus on the signal, not the noise. Delegate as much as you can, minimize the rest of it.

9. *Delegate!* You are only as productive as your team, so delegate as much as you dare and perhaps even more.

When you delegate well, you will discover:

- Your team may well come up with better solutions than you identified.
- You will have more time to focus on where you will make the most difference.
- Your team will become more skilled and capable as they take on more challenging tasks.
- Your team will be more motivated to perform well when they have real responsibility and autonomy, instead of being micro-managed.
- Because you trust your team, they will trust you and want to perform for you. They may even rate you well in your next 360-degree review.

These are serious benefits to offset the perceived loss of control that goes with delegation. Good delegation and good leadership march hand in hand.

31

Know your role

The challenge

Forests have been destroyed by all the books and articles which explore the role of the leader. Effective delegation raises an existential question for leaders. If you delegate everything, is there anything left for you to do? Or do you delegate yourself out of a job?

Once you have delegated everything you can, you are left with the essence of your leadership job.

In practice, as you become more senior you focus on less and less. I see this most obviously working with start-ups which succeed. At the outset, the founder is by default the CEO. She is also the IT help desk, receptionist, chief financial officer, book keeper, sales person and everything else. As the start-up grows, these tasks gradually get outsourced or delegated to a growing team. The CEO slowly transforms herself. She starts out as the jack of all trades, slowly becomes a manager and eventually becomes the leader focused on the IPM (Idea, People, Money and Machine) agenda. Her title, CEO, never changes but her role changes out of all recognition.

You face the same challenge as the start-up CEO. Regardless of your title, you have to keep on reinventing and redefining your role as you progress. In practice, that means you increasingly focus on the essence of leadership: you do less, but with more impact.

You have to keep on reinventing and redefining your role

The solution

To discover the solution, go back to basics. A leader is someone who takes people where they would not have got by themselves. That means the essence of leadership lies in the IPM agenda (chapter 32):

- Idea: set the direction and strategy. This is where you will make a difference and take people where they would not have got by themselves.
- People: recruit the right people to execute the strategy.
- Money and Machine. Secure the resources you need to succeed. Build the rhythms and routines of success so you can manage the day-to-day noise but still achieve your goals.

At a high level, the IPM agenda helps set your priorities and focus. But that still leaves open the question of what you should actually do all day? This is where the delegation challenge provides the answer, and it is worth repeating here because it is so important. The main tasks of the leader on a day-to-day basis all support the IPM agenda and are:

1. *Setting strategy and direction.* But gain insight and support from customers, stakeholders, support staff, colleagues and your team.
2. *Recruiting your team.* Let your team advise you on who is best, and to help sell the role. Use HR to support the process.
3. *Performance management and assessments.* HR can run the process, and self-assessment is often best.
4. *Negotiating and managing budgets.* Set your team up for success with the right budget and resource.
5. *Running interference.* Protect your team from unnecessary top management and reporting demands.
6. *Focus on one key project or priority.* Know where you will have your claim to fame this year, and focus on that.
7. *Delegate.* You are only as productive as your team, so delegate as much as you dare, and beyond.
8. *Coaching your team.* Delegation does not mean abandoning your team. Coach them to success, where they want help.
9. *Dealing with noise.* But don't mistake activity for achievement. Delegate or minimize the noise of day-to-day routine: stay focused on your IPM agenda.

PART FIVE

LEADING ORGANIZATIONS

32

Take control

The challenge

You cannot lead if you are not in control. Control can be highly elusive, at any level of the organization. In the middle of an organization it is standard to face conflicting pressures and priorities, to have responsibility which exceeds your authority and to have insufficient time, money and resources. Even at senior levels, you are not truly in control if you are executing someone else's agenda, or if you are simply administering the legacy you inherited from your predecessor.

Lack of control leads to poor performance and high stress.

- Poor performance. Loss of control puts you at the mercy of other people's agendas. You will find yourself constantly fighting battles about which priorities come first, and you will be juggling demands on your time and the time of your team.
- Stress. Loss of control leads directly to stress. You may respond well to pressure: a deadline is a useful call to arms. But when you have pressure, but lack control, the result is stress. If you now have the pressure of a deadline but you are dependent on third parties who do not share your sense of pressure, suddenly you are powerless and anxiety levels will go through the roof.

If you do not control your destiny, someone else will

If you do not control your destiny, someone else will.

The solution

Here is a simple formula for taking control: IPM. IPM stands for:

1. Idea
2. People
3. Money and Machine

If you have IPM in place, you are more than halfway to success. Without IPM, you have not even started the journey to success. Use IPM to check whether you are set up for success or not.

1. Idea

Your idea is how you will demonstrate the art of leadership, which is:

'to take people where they would not have got by themselves'

If you do not have a clear idea of what you want to achieve in your role, you will be at the mercy of other people's priorities and plans. A good idea tells a simple story which helps everyone in your team and beyond understand what you are doing and how you are making a difference.

A good idea will look like RUSSIA, which stands for:

- *Relevant.* Your idea will address a relevant challenge or opportunity, and it will be relevant to the broader agenda of your boss and the firm as a whole.
- *Unique.* Your idea will be unique to your team and your time: it will show how you are making a difference.
- *Simple.* If your idea has 38 elements to it, it will be highly sophisticated. But no one will be able to remember it or act on it. The best ideas are very simple and stretching: 'put a man on the moon by the end of this decade and bring him back alive again' (President Kennedy).
- *Stretching.* Taking people where they would not have got by themselves implies stretch. By stretching your team they will grow and learn, if you support them well. No stretch implies that you are simply an administrator of what is already there.

- *Impactful.* Your idea must make a difference which has impact and is noticed not just by your team, but across the organization. If it has real impact, your idea will be a claim to fame which boosts your career. Dare to be bold.
- *Actionable.* Everyone in your team must know what they are meant to do to help you achieve the idea. This sense of accountability can be empowering and motivating: it is your chance to show how each team member has an important role to play and makes an important contribution.

Your idea does not have to be a moon shot. It can be very simple such as:

- Become customer friendly
- Move to remote working/digital working/global working
- Achieve six sigma quality
- Be fastest to market with new products
- Be lowest cost

Your one simple idea will then be the focus for many other ideas and initiatives which will help you achieve that one big, simple idea.

2. People
You are only as good as your team. Selecting and developing the right team was covered in chapter 25. There are three principles to hold on to:

- Don't compromise when hiring. A weak team member means you and your team have to deal with the consequences of poor performance. You will eventually need to move the team member out, with inevitably difficult conversations and conflict. It is a recipe for stress, overwork and long nights which can be avoided by making the right hire in the first place.
- Hire to values, not just skills. You can always train skills, but you can never train values. People problems are normally about values, not about skills.
- Hire diversely. Avoid group think. You need people on your team with different skills, attitudes, perspectives and ways of thinking. This leads to better decision making and better balance across the

team. Within this diversity, you need to identify the three values which you will not compromise on.

3. Money and Machine

As a manager you have to control your budget and make your machine work. Your machine must have all the right rhythms and routines for:

- Reporting
- Communication
- Budget control
- Project management
- Performance management

These routines matter. They enable your team to structure their working day and week; they let you achieve control with minimum effort; they free up time for everyone to focus on delivering their work. Structure and predictability should be a scaffold around which your team can organize their work. Too much structure becomes a prison which prevents your team from performing. The best machine is a lean machine.

Money and machine hides two traps for the unwary manager.

- Inertia. You probably inherited a machine which worked more or less well. Do not assume that the machine which worked in the past is fit for the future. If you simply run the machine you inherited, you are an administrator of a legacy handed down to you. As a manager, you have to show that you can change and improve the legacy you inherited.
- Priorities. IPM should be tackled in that order. Idea comes first, because that dictates who you need on your team and what sort of machine you need to achieve your goal. People come second: great people will make a mediocre machine work well, but a weak team will struggle however good your machine is. Many weak managers prefer to avoid the difficult challenges of finding the right idea and people, instead, they tinker with the machine. It looks managerial and it shows that you are doing something, but it achieves little. Never mistake activity for achievement.

33

Make change happen

The challenge

As a leader, you have to take people where they would not have got by themselves. That means you have to make change happen. It is not enough to sustain or improve a legacy you inherited in your role: that is what all managers have to do. Even sustaining a legacy is very hard work. It is not enough to improve things: you have to change things and do things differently.

The myth of the stable baseline shows how hard it is to sustain things, let alone change them. Firms initiate endless change initiatives to reduce costs, improve revenues and grow market share. Even if the initiatives all succeed, the firm finds that neither their profits nor their market share has grown. The problem is the declining baseline. Managers assume that there is a stable baseline which means that cost cuts improve profits and market initiatives raise market share.

The reality is that the baseline of firm performance, profits and market share is always declining. However hard you try, competitors are trying at least as hard as you are. In addition, customers want more for less, suppliers offer less for more, the taxman and regulators just want more and within the firm, skilled people leave and new people join. The forces of entropy conspire against you.

Change is the real test of a good leader

If you are to succeed with change, you have to overcome the declining baseline; you have to deal with the forces of entropy and inertia within the firm which work against you; you have to overcome politics and passive and overt resistance.

Change is the real test of a good leader. This section shows how you can set yourself up to succeed in that test.

The solution

Most change efforts, like most battles, succeed or fail before they start. The effort you put into setting up your change initiative may be only 5–10 per cent of the total effort of the change programme, but will determine 80–90 per cent of the success of the effort. If you set yourself up the wrong way, you set yourself up to fail. Effort spent in planning and preparing your change initiative is rarely wasted.

Over the years, a simple formula has proven to be an uncanny predictor of whether a change effort will succeed or fail. Here it is:

$$N \times V \times C \times F > R$$

Where:

- N = need for change
- V = vision for the change
- C = capability and capacity for change
- F = first steps
- R = risks and costs of change

Here is how to use the change equation in practice.

Need for change

The need to change is both corporate and personal.

Where there is pain, there is a need for change. If there is no pain, it is hard to make change happen. Most people do not like change, even if they pretend that they like it. Change involves personal risk: I may be asked to work harder, have new and challenging goals, work for a different boss, acquire new skills: so what's in it for me? Most people understand that they need to say that they are in favour

Where there is pain, there is a need for change

of change. They will not want to be seen to sabotage change actively. Instead, they will passively resist it. Doing nothing is a very good form of resistance: it is hard to overcome the inertia of the organization.

To counter this, you need to show that there is a real personal need for change. Show that the risk of doing nothing is greater than the risk of changing. This is what CEOs like to call 'the burning platform'. If I invited you to spend a freezing night in an open boat in the middle of the Atlantic in winter, you would probably decline my offer, especially if you were used to the first-class lifestyle. And yet first-class people were fighting for the privilege of taking up this offer when they were passengers on the Titanic. If there is a real need for change, anyone will change. If there is no real need to change, expect passive resistance.

Fear often makes CEOs suckers for the latest management fad. If everyone else seems to be doing process re-engineering, or cloud computing, or blue ocean strategy then a CEO will not want to be left behind. Each fad promises to be transformational, with case histories giving implausible results. Following a fad is less risky than ignoring it: if you follow it and it flops, you are no worse off than your peers. If things go wrong and you have not followed the fad, you are left exposed to the charge that you failed to keep up with the times.

Pain and fear sells change: show that the pain of doing nothing is greater than the pain of making change happen.

Vision for the change

Like the need for change, the vision is both corporate and personal.

Your vision for change will come in the form of a business case for the firm. This will show measurable impact in terms of costs, revenues, profit, product quality, market share, time to market, customer retention, etc. A good business case unlocks the budget, resources and management support you need to make change happen. Without that, you have an idea which flounders.

Your vision also needs to win the hearts and minds of your colleagues and team members. This is where the vision becomes personal. You need to answer the WIFM question for them: 'What's In It For Me?' In practice, the vision which works for most people comes in one of three flavours:

- *Survival:* 'without this change effort, your role and job will become redundant.' This converts fear, implicit in the need for change, into the vision for change.
- *Control:* 'if you support this effort you have a chance to influence its outcome. Do you want to be on the outside when we decide who keeps their jobs and who loses their jobs?'
- *Advancement:* Change can be the chance to learn new skills and gain new experience to build a career in the middle of an organization.

At senior levels, staff see every restructuring as a chance to grab a better role at the expense of their colleagues. Change can become very political very fast.

The personal vision for change reveals an ugly truth about change: not everyone benefits from it. You will not please everyone and not everyone will support you. If you try to please everyone,

Change can become very political very fast

you will be letting opponents of change have a veto over your change idea. Instead, you have to build a coalition of the willing. Find enough support among the key decision makers and influencers to make change happen. When everyone else sees that change is going to happen, they will all decide accordingly. If you show that the train is going to leave the station, most people will get on board; some will stay on the platform and start to feel lonely (they will run after the train trying to catch it); a few die-hards will lie down on the tracks in front of the train to stop it. No matter: the train leaves the station. Don't let a minority stop you or derail you.

Capability and capacity for change

This is the acid test for any change programme. After you have established the need and the vision for change, the C-suite may tell you that you have their support. But support without commitment is worthless. You need commitment, not just support. You need budget, resources and skills to make your change happen. Because change is difficult, you need the best resources and skills: you are not going to succeed if the talent assigned to you is a mix of the untried and untested, plus some people who need a second or third chance.

This is the point at which you have to discover your ruthless side. Do not accept second best. Force the CEO and C-suite to look at what it takes to set the change up for success. You have to show that your vision and need for change is greater than all the other visions and needs in the firm. This conversation is fundamentally about priorities: the right budget and team is always available for the right priority. It is legitimate for the CEO to say that your idea is great, but not the top priority. It is then legitimate for you to walk away. Trying to change with an inadequate budget and team is a recipe for stress, sleepless nights and failure. It is not worth it.

Once you have the right budget and team, you need one more thing to ensure you have the capacity and capability to change. You need a powerful sponsor. The sponsor has a vital role which does not take much time. Your sponsor is the person who will manage politics for you, overcome high-level road blocks, give you access to decision makers and watch your back for you. In return, you have to make your sponsor look great with a great programme.

First steps
If you have the vision, need and capability and capacity for change you are well on the way to a successful start. But any change programme is vulnerable when it starts. Inevitably, when you start you will discover that the change is never as easy as you had planned. Unexpected obstacles will appear. This is your moment of maximum danger. There will be plenty of doubters who will be more than happy to show that your vision was pie in the sky and it will not work. Colleagues who joined your bandwagon because they thought it was the bandwagon to succeed will mysteriously vanish, and you will start to feel very lonely.

You need two things when you start: early wins and the commitment process.

Early wins are a way of showing that your bandwagon is moving and that it will succeed. It will not be yet another corporate initiative that quietly disappears. Early wins are small successes such as:

- Simple cost savings
- Market research which confirms your idea
- Preliminary technical work which demonstrates viability
- First cut designs for the new system, product, office etc.

Whatever these small gains may be, trumpet them loud and widely. Show that your bandwagon is moving, and slowly more people will want to join it.

The commitment process is about reinforcing the commitment of key players and demonstrating to the rest of the organization that the key players support you. When the C-suite backs your idea, there will be an initial flush of enthusiasm and goodwill from them. Use that goodwill, fast. Ask the CEO and others to record a video, hold a town hall meeting or send out an email discussing the change. This is their chance to show their leadership and it is your chance to turn their private commitment into a public commitment. This matters. If their commitment is private, it is weak: they can afford to see you fail. If they are committed in public, they are committed to your success: they do not want to be associated with a failure. Public commitment beats private commitment every time.

Risks and costs of change

Most firms have good procedures for managing risks. The risk log is a staple of C-suite and board meetings, complete with its risk ratings and mitigating actions. These sorts of risks are normally rational risks such as: 'what if we suffer a data breach, what if our key supplier lets us down?' Your change programme will probably also have a risk register. Because firms are familiar with such risks, they are relatively easy to deal with.

The real costs and risks of change are not rational. They are political and emotional. As we have seen in this chapter, change is risky for most people. Colleagues who fear your change will find all the rational reasons why it is risky and why it might fail. These arguments are a smokescreen for the real reason they oppose change: personal risk and fear. Fighting emotion with reason is like fighting fire with gas: entertaining, but not advisable.

If you argue the rational case in public, positions just become more entrenched. Instead, find time to talk to colleagues, influencers and stakeholders in private. A meeting is private when it is 1 to 1; it is public as soon as there is a third person in the room. In a private meeting you can find out what really motivates someone, and in private colleagues are more willing to change their position. All of this takes time and effort: it is a vital investment in setting your change up for success.

34

Manage projects

The challenge

Managing a project is the rational process through which you deliver change. Managing change is largely a political and emotional process of persuasion, with some vital rational elements. Change management and project management depend on each other.

Project management is a skill and an entire career in its own right. Your goal is not to become a qualified project manager. Your goal is to become a leader who makes change happen. As a leader you move from asking 'how can I do this?' to 'who can do this?' The good news is that there are many highly skilled project managers who can help you. You have to choose the right version to suit your needs. For instance, Agile project management has its origins in software development, whereas PRINCE2 is seen as a broader, more generic project management framework.

As a leader, you have to make sure that project management is a framework for success, not a **Move from asking 'how can I do this?' to 'who can do this?'**

prison of failure. At its worst, project management can become an end in itself. I have seen a project disappear into irrelevance as it created risk logs, issue logs, activity logs, telephone logs, meeting logs, master logs and more: everything was being logged, nothing was being achieved. At its best, a good project manager will help you:

- Keep control: know what needs to happen when, and if it actually happens
- Accelerate progress: identify the critical path of the required order of events

- Create simplicity out of complexity: cut the project into bite-sized slices
- Manage risk and identify and pre-empt problems

The simple solution to managing a complex project is to hire a good project manager. But many projects are not that complex: you will have to manage them yourself. And even if you have a project manager, you need to be able to ask him or her the right questions. This chapter shows how you can do this.

The solution

Good project management is about how you get any task done: the same principles apply if you are preparing a report or building a nuclear power plant. This solution starts with how you manage a project that you alone should work on; it will then show how you can deal with the complexity of managing multiple work streams and people. The principles of task and project management are:

1. Start at the end
2. Break the complex task down into bite-sized chunks
3. Find the critical path for your project
4. Identify and deal with potential risks and obstacles
5. Monitor progress and establish governance

1. Start at the end
Perhaps the worst advice ever given to leaders is 'first things first'. If you start from here you commit to a random walk where you react to whatever happens next. The better advice is 'start at the end'. Be clear about the outcome you want. Danger arises when you want to achieve many things. If you shoot at three targets at the same time, you can be guaranteed to miss them all. Force yourself and your team to be clear about the one main goal you must achieve: there may be other minor benefits you want as well, but stay focused on what matters most. Focus will give you clear priorities and will ensure decision making about resources and actions is much easier for you.

2. Break the complex task down into bite-sized chunks
At the outset, any worthwhile project will seem daunting: there is too much to do. Your first job is to understand what is the minimum work required to

achieve the task. Then break down the large task into a series of small tasks. For instance, writing a book on leadership is a huge task: where do you start and what do you write? By breaking leadership down into 44 constituent elements, all following a consistent structure, it is possible to write the book one bite-sized chunk at a time.

This is where you can drown in detail, because there is so much to be done. At pain of repetition, focus on the minimum number of steps required to achieve your goal. If there are seven steps, you then focus on the first step. You can then repeat the exercise: what is the minimum number of actions required to accomplish the first step? Continue drilling down until you have clarity about what you need to do today (a good bite-sized chunk of work) and what you will do tomorrow. You will be able to see how these small pieces of work lead to achieving your much larger project.

3. Find the critical path for your project

The critical path identifies which actions depend on others: you cannot start on decorating before your new house until you have put in the foundations of the building, for instance. This sequencing may seem obvious, but unless you do it well it can trip you up. While there may be things you should obviously start work on, there may well be some iceberg tasks which could sink you. These are tasks which are not immediately obvious and necessary, but become important later on. If, for instance, you need a minor but vital input from a supplier in three months' time, it is tempting to leave that for at least two more months. But if the supplier works on a three-month delivery lead time, that routine input suddenly becomes an urgent task.

No plan survives first contact with reality

4. Identify and deal with potential risks and obstacles

No plan survives first contact with reality. As world boxing champion Mike Tyson put it: 'Everyone has a plan until they get punched in the mouth.' It is easy to look at the future with rose-tinted spectacles: we all tend to assume things will work out for the best. While it is good to hope for the best, plan for the worst: surprises are rarely good. For every risk, you should identify a mitigating action which will either prevent the risk happening, or deal with the risk should it happen. By doing this in advance, you reduce the likelihood that fate will conspire to throw you off course. You will still be faced by surprises, but there will be fewer of them and you can stay in control of events.

5. Monitor progress and establish governance

The two traps here are: too much monitoring and too little monitoring.

Some projects suffer death by oversight. If they are important and visible, everyone wants to know what is going on. Senior managers can often be at fault here: they like to ask for onerous and excessively frequent reports, update meetings and project reviews. Different senior managers and departments may also ask for bespoke reports which meet their particular needs.

Other projects drift in the absence of oversight. It is too easy to assume that the team is in control and that they will tell you if they need help or if anything goes wrong. The problem with that is that when they tell you they need help, it may well be too late. Never assume anything. Regular check-ups are good for your personal health, and they are good for your project: you never know what you might find.

Never assume anything

The solution is to agree who will monitor progress (you or a steering group); how often reports will be made and what they will look like. Do this properly and you will create an effective governance system which not only monitors progress, but can make timely decisions as well. Reporting without decision making is a bureaucratic waste of time: reporting and decision making should always be linked.

35

Grow your influence across the organization

The challenge

Formal power is not enough to sustain your leadership journey. In the past, your power was defined by your budget and span of control. More money and more staff meant more power. Money and staff still matter, but they are not enough. If you are to succeed, you need the help and support of people outside your control: other departments, top management, contractors and customers. Your informal power multiplies your formal power dramatically, and will often lead to you being given more formal power as well.

Chapter 24 showed how you can build influence with individuals. This chapter shows how you can build influence across the organization as a whole.

The solution

Just as there is no single point solution for becoming a smart leader, so there is no single point solution for becoming influential. There is no magic sauce, or if there is then someone is hiding it very well.

Instead, influence involves a suite of actions and behaviours that transforms you from being a cog in the machine to be a leader who influences and changes the machine. Below are six of the most important actions and behaviours you need to build your influence.

Most careers are built on a claim to fame

1. *Have a claim to fame*. Most careers are built on a claim to fame. At the start of a career, your claim to fame may be as simple as working for a blue chip and prestigious firm. Like attending a top business school, it is a lifelong quality mark: future employers know that you have been pre-selected as a high potential individual. At some point in your career, you need to be known for achieving something: you introduced a new product, re-organized a business, saved a business from collapse or introduced a whole new way of doing things in your area of expertise. The bigger your claim to fame, the better. Your success demonstrates that you can succeed with the toughest challenges. Your reward will be to have the chance of taking on even bigger and even more challenging opportunities. Your informal power is your rocket fuel which launches you towards more formal power.

2. *Stake your claim*. If failure is a lonely place, then success is very crowded. You not only need a claim to fame, you need to stake your claim because plenty of other people will be more than happy to steal the credit for your success. Do not be shy and do not hide your light under a bushel. You have endless opportunities to gently remind everyone about your success. For example, in discussion you can draw on what you learned from your experience: 'what I learned when I/we launched the new product was.....'

Ultimately, you need to build and control a narrative about who you are. You probably struggle to identify how many of your colleagues have succeeded, and they will struggle to identify why you are special. A big claim to fame means that they will always know you as the person who launched the product/saved the business/started that new way of doing things. Your claim to fame helps you both inside your current organization, but is also very persuasive when you want a new role: it helps you stand out against all the other candidates who will also be very talented. It is proof positive that you can put your talent to good use.

If failure is a lonely place, then success is very crowded

3. *Step up, not step back*. There are moments of truth in every firm when power visibly ebbs and flows between managers. These

moments of truth are often moments of crisis when no one is quite sure what to do. Followers step back to see which way things go: that is a low-risk survival strategy. Where others see risk, leaders see opportunity to make a difference, to learn, to grow and to establish a claim to fame. By definition, you do not know when a crisis will erupt or why. But you know that at some point, a crisis will occur. See chapter 37 on how you can prepare for the unexpected crisis, so that you can make the most of it.

4. *Become the leader people want to follow*, not the leader they have to follow. It is unusual to be a boss that people actually want to work for. It is a claim to fame based on your style, not your performance. But it is still powerful. Once the grapevine starts to hear that you are the sort of boss that is worth working for, everyone will start to see you more positively. Top performers will want to work for you, helping you sustain even better performance. Colleagues and even bosses will see you as an effective manager: impressions matter.

5. *Build your network of trust.* You need to make things happen through people you do not control. You can do that to some extent on a transactional basis by using your powers of persuasion to get their support and agreement. As a leader, you need to move from a series of one-off transactions with each colleague to building a relationship based on trust. Just as you need to be the leader people want to follow, you need to be the colleague others want to work with. How you build trust was covered in chapter 24.

6. *Act the part and look the part.* As you think of all your colleagues, you may not know how well they are rated in their performance assessment. But you will have a very vivid idea about what they are like: how they act **Style should not** and how they look. Confident people are **matter, but it does** often mistaken for being competent people. You will search your employee handbook in vain for a style guide to success. In practice, the guide is staring you in the face all day. Observe how people one or two levels above you behave and dress: the rules will be different for different functions, firms and

countries. But the unwritten rules will be very clear: follow them. If you want to join their club, you have to act and look like you are part of the club. It is possible that you look at how they act and you may decide that is not how you want to be or behave: that is a good moment to start looking for a role elsewhere.

36

Fighting battles

The challenge

Organizations are set up for conflict. This is a surprise to organizational theorists, but not a surprise to anyone who works in an organization. Every organization is full of competing factions with different agendas and priorities. Each business unit wants more resource; finance, IT, marketing, sales and HR all correctly believe that they have a vital role; none of them want to get by with less resource or priority.

Most of the time there is constructive competition between all these groups: to perform the best, to promote their own agenda and needs and to secure the resources and support they need to succeed.

Organizations are set up for conflict

Even within a team, each team member has different responsibilities and perspectives. In a high-functioning team, there is constructive dissent. Different views are valuable because you are more likely to find the best solution when there are multiple options than when there is just one option: the view of the boss.

Occasionally, constructive competition becomes unconstructive warfare and constructive dissent becomes an argument. The challenge is to know when and how to fight internal corporate battles.

The solution

The solution to this challenge is 2,500 years old and is provided by Chinese philosopher Sun Tzu in the classic text *The Art of War*. He outlined three conditions under which you should choose to fight:

- Only fight when there is a prize worth fighting for
- Only fight when you know you will win
- Only fight when there is no other way of achieving your aims

Most corporate battles fail at least one, and often all three, of the criteria above. Not only are they a waste of time; they are pointless. It is usually better to win a friend than to win a battle. If you win a friend, then you can win the argument because it is easier to persuade a friend than an enemy. Even if you win the battle, you have earned an enemy, which will hurt you at a later date.

Here is how to apply Sun Tzu's three rules of warfare to your organization:

Only fight when there is a prize worth fighting for

Some of the biggest battles are over the smallest things. I have seen boards shed blood over choosing the new corporate typeface and whether staff should be given a celebration drink. These are battles where everyone can have an opinion and pretend to have knowledge. On far more substantive issues, such as which IT platform shall we consolidate on to at a cost of $100 million, there is only one expert at the table and so there is no argument.

Let others fight over the corporate typeface. It probably is not even worth arguing over the IT platform, unless you can see the choice directly affects your ability to meet your goals. For a prize to be worth fighting for it has to be a big prize (like the choice of IT platform) but it also has to be relevant to you. Battles which are worth fighting include:

- Agreeing your goals
- Securing the right team
- Negotiating the right budget

These are fundamental to your success. Ideally, you get what you want without a battle. But if you have to fight, make sure you win.

Only fight when you know you will win

Sun Tzu understood that most battles are won or lost before they start. One side will have amassed all the allies and support to assure success, the other side will not. You need to do the same. Prepare your case and build your allies in advance. If you find you have all the allies and arguments on your side, you can proceed with confidence. Any opposition will quietly melt away. If you find that your arguments are not producing the allies you need, then you know you are on weak ground. This is your moment to melt away. Either you need to change your arguments, or you need to fight a different battle.

Only fight when there is no other way of achieving your aims

Wartime leader Winston Churchill remarked 'jaw-jaw is better than war-war': talking is better than fighting. The key is to talk the right way. Too often conversations are set up as a win/lose conversation. They become war-war in the form of jaw-jaw. They are win/lose conversations.

The classic win/lose conversation is the sales discussion over price: the buyer wants a lower price and the seller wants a higher price. Where's a win/win in that discussion? **'Jaw-jaw is better** With creativity, you can turn even this discussion **than war-war'** into a win/win. Perhaps you can offer a lower price, if the buyer agrees to buy a larger volume, or to feature your product prominently in store, or agrees to pay up front, or agrees to pay on low monthly instalments (with a higher overall price), or perhaps you can add in service or insurance at low cost.

Avoiding war-war usually requires very creative jaw-jaw. Identify a win for the other side and change the terms of the discussion, as in the price negotiation above. Be creative in your jaw-jaw or be prepared for war-war.

37

Turn crises into opportunities

The challenge

Crises are inevitable in any leadership career and in any organization. If you have never had a crisis in a 40 year career, you have never led. By definition, you do not know when the crisis will come or what it will be. Despite that, you can still prepare for them. Although each crisis is unique, there are predictable patterns of failure and success in how you respond to the crisis.

This section looks at how you can turn a crisis into an opportunity. Every crisis is a moment of truth which can make or break your career. Make the most of it.

The solution

You will be judged not just by what you do in a crisis, but by how you are. Style counts for at least as much as substance. Think back to some crises you have experienced or observed. It is hard to remember exactly who did what and when. But you will remember vividly what people were like: some will have seemed to be part of the solution, and others will have seemed to be part of the problem.

Style counts for at least as much as substance

This section looks at how you can respond with both a winning style and substance to your next crisis.

Style

You already know what a good style looks like. Think back to various crises you have seen and remember how different people reacted. You will remember some positively, others negatively. The chances are that the differences will look something like the table below. It is easy to display at least some of the negative symptoms during a crisis. It takes real effort to display all the positive symptoms below.

Crisis as opportunity	Crisis as a problem
Project hope, certainty and clarity	Project fear, doubt and confusion
Positive and supportive	Negative and blaming
Calm	Panic
Drive to action	Analyse what went wrong
Show empathy	No empathy, plenty of blaming
Decisive	Vague, ambiguous, uncertain

Complete your own list of what you think good and bad looks like in a crisis. Keep that note and when the next crisis occurs, pull the note out to remind yourself about how you want to be seen and remembered. This is the first step to success: know that you always have a choice about how you behave. Behave the way you want to be remembered.

During a crisis, you will rediscover the principle of wearing the mask of leadership. It is likely that you will be feeling anxiety, fear, frustration and doubt. If you make your feelings known, your little cloud of gloom will spread like a major depression across your team and firm. Your gloom will become self reinforcing, as your team becomes gloomier and more ineffective, which will make you gloomier and a vicious circle is quickly established. This is the moment to remember that leaders are peddlers of hope, certainty and clarity especially when there appears to be little hope, certainty and clarity.

Behave the way you want to be remembered

Substance

If your crisis becomes a disaster, it does not matter how stylish you are: you will fail. As with the style response it is both obvious and difficult to respond the right way to a crisis. The highlights are in the table below and then briefly explained:

Crisis as opportunity	Crisis as a problem
Recognize the challenge	Deny the challenge
Step up	Step back and hide
Drive to action hard and fast	Hide behind analysis
Control your destiny: be decisive	Wait for others to decide
Get help	Be the lone hero
Control the narrative	Under-communicate
Spread the praise	Claim all the credit

Here is how you can put the principles above into practice:

1. *Recognize the challenge*
A common reaction to a problem is to deny it and hope it disappears. Problems rarely go away or solve themselves.

Reacting the right way is a mindset challenge. Think of the challenge positively: it is a chance to prove yourself. Make it your mission to stay in control and achieve a great outcome.

2. *Step up*
At moments of crisis, followers step back and leaders step up. Stepping back is safe: you can see which way the wind is blowing and then follow the crowd. No one was sacked for following the crowd. Stepping up accelerates your career: you succeed fast or you fail fast. But the more you step up, the better you become at taking responsibility and learning to deal with crises well. Use every chance to step up and you will become expert at crisis management, and your calmness will be natural, not an act. By stepping up, you make yourself the leader whatever your official title may be. Stepping up can be as simple as volunteering an idea: you may well be asked to put your idea into action.

3. *Drive to action, hard and fast*
Followers prefer analysis to action, and political players prefer to spread the blame and duck responsibility. Both those reactions will allow the crisis to spiral out of control. The earlier you deal with the problem, the easier it is to deal with.

4. *Control your destiny: be decisive*
If you don't control your destiny, someone else will. They will not have your best interests at heart. If you don't make decisions, someone else will. You

will be the victim of fate, not the master of fate. Making decisions in a crisis is never easy because all crises suffer from VUCA: they are volatile, uncertain, complex and ambiguous. VUCA is your friend, not your enemy. Because of VUCA no one is sure what to do: this allows you to be assertive and push your decision and your priorities with minimal opposition. Followers will be grateful for the clarity that a decision gives, because it helps them drive to action. Action gives them hope that things will get better.

5. *Get help*
You cannot succeed alone. You need help for at least four reasons:

- Make things happen: you do not have enough hours in the day to do it all yourself. Make sure you get the resources, budget and support you need.
- Provide political air cover. Politics can erupt in a highly dysfunctional way during a crisis: the blame game starts, people start positioning themselves to take advantage. You need at least one power baron or baroness who will mind your back so that you can focus on the task in hand. This sponsor is unlikely to appear out of thin air in the heat of the crisis. Cultivate your sponsor in the good times, so that you have a powerful ally in the tough times.
- Give advice and support. Many people will be offering their opinions. You need a few trusted advisors who can help you separate the signal from the noise and give you impartial advice on what to do.
- Provide moral and emotional support. In a crisis many people will be looking to you for moral support: they may be feeling anxious, tired or frustrated. It is exhausting to carry this emotional burden as well as dealing with the rational and political battles of a crisis. You may have a confidante at work you can lean on but more likely you need to be able to lean on family, friends or a professional coach.

6. *Control the narrative*
It is easy to be so focused on fighting the fire that communicating seems like a luxury, not a necessity. This is a mistake. When a crisis hits, gossip on the grapevine goes into overdrive. In the absence of a clear narrative, people start creating their own narratives. These will often be melodramatic and unhelpful. The principle is simple: if you don't fill the void, others will.

If in doubt, over-communicate

Since everyone wants to know what is going on, tell them. If in doubt, over-communicate. In particular, make sure that all the key decision makers understand the narrative from your perspective. If you let them create their own narrative, you may suddenly find that they have also created their own agenda: you will have lost control of the narrative, the agenda and your destiny. That is not a good place to be.

In practice, you will find that most of your time is spent communicating, influencing and persuading: you need a team for all the doing.

7. *Spread the praise*

At the moment of victory it is tempting to bask in the limelight and accept the plaudits. You can do that, but you can do something even better. Instead of taking all the praise, give it all away. This does two very powerful things for you:

- You build your personal influence. Few people dislike being praised. Your colleagues will appreciate your praise. Human nature is to want to reciprocate: your generosity will be repaid in the future.
- You demonstrate that you were the leader in the crisis. Many people will try to steal the credit for success. By giving away all the credit, you demonstrate that you are the person who knows who did what and that you were at the centre of the response. You take credit by giving it away.

PART SIX

LEADING STRATEGY

38

How to have a strategic conversation

The challenge

Strategy has come to mean important, with bells on: think of strategic initiatives, or even the latest floor plan strategy. Although the word is much misused and greatly misunderstood, strategy matters. The strategy of your firm is how it will achieve its goals; it is the framework which helps the firm decide where to allocate resources and which priorities to pursue. At a personal level, your strategy is how you will achieve your goals and allocate your time and effort.

Strategy is hard. If it was simple, it would be easy for firms to survive: they would know how to achieve their goals profitably and competitively. But firms struggle to survive. The average life span of a firm in the S&P500 is now 18 years, down from 61 years **Strategy is hard** in 1958. The forces of creative destruction are becoming more destructive, if not more creative. The pace of competition is heating up and the challenge of strategy is becoming greater than ever. Good strategy is now a matter of basic survival.

Becoming an expert at strategy can cost a fortune in business school fees and make you a fortune as a strategy consultant. But your goal is not to be the expert; it is to be the leader. As leader, you do not need to be the smartest person in the room: you need to bring the smartest people into the room.

Once you have the strategy experts in the room, you need to know how to get the best out of them. You need to have a good strategic conversation. That is the focus of this chapter.

The solution

Fortunately, there is a tried and tested formula for a good strategic conversation. This formula has traditionally been used by the leading strategy consulting firms to test potential recruits to the firm. It is called the case study interview. Use this formula and you can have a good strategy conversation with the experts, or you could even join a top strategy firm.

Ask smart questions before attempting to arrive at smart answers

The goal of the case study interview is to take an ambiguous but challenging strategy problem ('should we enter the Thai tapioca market' for instance) and work out a plausible solution. You resolve this by looking at the problem from at least six angles. At every stage, you need to ask smart questions before attempting to arrive at smart answers.

Market perspective

How big is the market overall, and is it growing or declining? This is not as obvious as it sounds. For instance, how big is the car market? Well it depends: which countries do you include, are you looking at traditional ICE cars, hybrid cars or electric cars; are you including luxury cars and small runabouts for town? Quickly, you find you have to move from talking about 'the market' to the 'target market' or 'served market'. Your choice of target market may be fundamental to your future survival and success.

Customer perspective

Great strategy starts with understanding what your customer wants. The key principles are:

- Different types of customer want different things and will pay different prices: customer segmentation is essential. Will you serve the luxury or economy segment of the market, for instance?
- Match what you offer to what your customer values. Staying at an economy hotel you will value cleanliness, quiet and a good bed for a good sleep. You will not value a fancy lobby, spa and rooftop bar. If you run a budget hotel, invest in what the customer values, and ignore what is not required.

- The customer is not always right, for two reasons. First, they do not always know what they want: no one knew they wanted social media until it was offered and they were hooked. Second, even if they tell you, they may be wrong out of politeness or confusion. If you want to find out what customers really want, watch the feet not the mouth: track behaviour, not opinions.
- The larger the organization, the more the voice of the customer is lost. This is your chance to make a difference by listening to the customer and reacting appropriately.

Channels

How are you going to reach your customers and at what cost? You can go direct, in which case you will need to build your brand strategy and work out how to get your message to your target customers: this leads on to the need for an advertising strategy (what is our message and to whom?) and to a media strategy (TV, paid search, print advertising etc.). Alternatively you can work through partners and distributors who

Leaders don't like competing: they like winning

will take their margin, and you lose control of the end customer: it becomes harder to hear your end customer when someone else is standing between you and the customer.

Competition

Leaders don't like competing: they like winning. That means that the best fight is an unfair fight, which you know you will win. The problem with a fair fight is that you might lose it. Competitive advantage is weak: you need a source of thoroughly unfair competitive advantage, for instance:

- Patents (pharmaceutical firms)
- Unmatchable network effects (Google, Microsoft)
- Lowest cost source of production (some oil majors with the best fields)
- Scale economies (next-generation chip production, Intel, TSMC, Samsung)
- Well-established brands (P&G, Diageo, Unilever)

A test of your competitive advantage is your profitability. If you struggle to make profits, you have no competitive advantage. If you are wildly profitable in one or two areas, you probably have high competitive advantage in those areas. The chances are that you are somewhere in the middle. In this greyspace, it is worth asking how sustainable your advantage is, for instance:

- Price advantage: lasts as long as it takes for competition to follow your price, unless you are the lowest cost provider in which case you can sustain low prices indefinitely.
- Product innovation: how long will it take for your competitor to copy you?
- Branding: how long will it take for competitors to build a rival brand? Clearly, a brand advantage is stickier than a price advantage.

Finally, your biggest competitive threat may not be plotting your downfall from the boardroom in a downtown skyscraper. She may be plotting your downfall from a garage in her parent's house in the suburbs. The most dangerous competitors are the new ones who completely change the rules of the game.

Organization

What unique skills and capabilities do we have? All firms like to think that they are good at something and may well call it a 'core competence'. It is not enough to be good at something: rest assured that your competitors will also think they are good at it. If you want your organization to be a source of competitive advantage, you need a genuine core competence which is both market beating and very hard to copy. Arguably, TSMC have a core competence in the manufacturing of advanced chips at 5nm and 3nm scale; Tesla has been creating a core competence in electric batteries, charging systems and autonomous driving (although many other firms want to catch up) and P&G has been building a core competence in branding for over 100 years (and many other firms have more or less caught up). Creating a core competence takes exceptional effort, but can drive exceptional rewards.

Financial perspective

This is the acid test of the strategy: is it profitable? If you work in the not for profit sector, the equivalent question is 'does it achieve our goals?' In practice, you have to look beyond one simple measure of profitability and look at a range of metrics:

- What is our profit margin, and how easily can it be competed away?
- How stable are our revenues? Do we depend on one or two contracts with one or two major customers such as government, in which case how do manage that risk?
- How sticky are our customers and how easy is it for them to switch? (most bank customers are more likely to switch spouse than switch bank, for instance).
- What is our return on capital? (or on investment, or equity depending on the measures used): this looks at the capital intensity of a project. High capital intensity could make cash flow a challenge, but may also make it harder for new entrants to enter the market.
- What does our cash flow look like? Some businesses are cash positive: you generate cash as you grow. For instance, retailers get paid by consumers before they pay their suppliers, so their growth need not consume cash. Building a new semiconductor plant (or nuclear plant or finding a new drug) costs billions and takes years before you see a penny of return.
- How does profitability and cash flow vary by market segment and are we in the right segments? Overall, do we have a balanced portfolio of products: some which are growing but consuming cash, some which are mature, profitable and generating cash and some in between? If all our businesses are generating cash and mature, then do we have any long-term future? On the other hand, if all our businesses are growing and consuming cash, where will we find the cash to fund the growth?

You will find all of these questions simply prompt more questions. You have to keep digging and keep exploring to craft a strategy which works for you. The discussion process is not a waste of time: it is the method by which you can clarify and hone your strategy.

The brutal reality is that most great strategies do not come from detailed strategy work: they come from a single great insight or a single bold idea which blows away all the detailed analysis. Tesla, Facebook and Google did not start with a detailed strategic analysis, because there was no market to analyse. They started with a bold idea. How you can practically develop a strategy for your organization is covered in chapter 40.

39

The language of strategy

The challenge

It is hard to have a strategy conversation if you do not know the language of strategy. Unfortunately, it is possible to drown in strategy jargon. Strategy jargon is used not to solve the problem, it is used to make the speaker feel smart and look smart. As a result, most strategy concepts are poorly understood and poorly used.

The purpose of this chapter is not to make you a strategy expert. It is to help you avoid drowning in strategy jargon. Used well, you will find that many of these concepts are of real use to you.

The solution

Here is an abbreviated A–Z of the top ten strategy concepts, and a note of the originator of each concept (where appropriate):

Blue ocean strategy (Chan Kim). Find an uncontested market and exploit it. It is easy to win when there is no competition. Best for start-ups; legacy firms in established markets struggle with this. A variation is to find a new way of competing in an existing market by understanding your customers' value curve (see below).

It is easy to win when there is no competition

Co-creation (Venkat Ramaswamy). Use your customers and suppliers to help you create your next generation product / service because they have the real insights about what is needed and what is possible. Co-creation is more than a survey and some market research: it involves pulling customers actively into your development and planning processes.

Core competence (CK Prahalad and Gary Hamel). A real core competence is something at which your firm excels; your competition will struggle to copy because it is more about tacit skills than explicit knowledge which can be put in a manual; is competitively relevant. Tesla is building core competence in batteries and autonomous driving: others may catch up but it will cost a fortune and take time. Core competence is now used to refer to anything we think we might do passably well: that completely misses the point because your competition probably do it just as well as you do.

Five Forces (Michael Porter) which are used to assess the strength of your competitive position. Your competitive position is strong if:

- Your immediate *market rivals* are weak, perhaps because you have network effects on your side (Microsoft desktop operating system, or your local water company for instance).
- Your *buyers* have weak bargaining power. Suppliers to supermarkets often struggle because they are weak compared to their buyer, the supermarket. Customers may have weak bargaining power with their mobile phone company, but they can switch easily. Ease of switching is a form of buyer power.
- Your *suppliers* have weak bargaining power. If you are a franchisee of McDonald's, or any other good franchise, you understand just how powerful a supplier can be: they will mandate exactly how you operate.
- There is a low threat of *new entrants*. New entrants into the advanced micro-chip business are unlikely: a new plant costs $20 billion to build, takes years and requires massive skills. The barriers to entry into starting a food stall at your local farmer's market are minimal.
- There are few *substitutes*, which are not always obvious. The substitute for a meal out might be a trip to the cinema, for instance. There may be no substitute for a life-saving drug, in which case expect to pay top dollar.

Portfolio Strategy (BCG Group). The key insight is that most firms are a portfolio of products and you need a balance between products which are growing (but need a lot of cash to support growth) and mature or declining (but are generating cash) to support the growth. This portfolio is often presented in a 2x2 matrix which may be called a BCG Grid or a growth/

share matrix. A close variation is to plot each part of your portfolio of businesses on another 2x2 grid which looks at the market attractiveness of each business (how fast the market is growing) and the competitive position of your business (its market share relative to competition).

Re-engineering (Champy and Hammer). Originally, this was a radical way of re-organizing the firm: do away with functional silos and organize around the processes which serve the customer best. It was intended to be highly customer focused. Re-engineering has now become cost cutting with a smile, where the smile is optional. It is an excuse for junior consultants to spend a fortune mapping all your processes in detail. Internal processes tend to become convoluted cow paths over time: an occasional spring cleaning is useful.

Strategic intent (CK Prahalad and Gary Hamel). In essence, this is an audacious goal which serves to focus all the efforts of the firm. In practice, it has often been used to challenge management to reach for the stars and to break away from business as usual. It is a useful way of issuing a call to arms, and is not intended as an analytic tool for strategy. It can be used to encourage blue-sky thinking about a radical new strategy.

The value chain gives you no idea where value is created

Value chain. In practice this looks at how cost builds up across a firm or an industry to deliver a final product to the customer e.g.: raw materials, production, financing, distribution, sales, overhead etc. It is useful for seeing where your costs go as opposed to the traditional functional and silo view of costs. You can score points in your strategy conversation by pointing out that the value chain gives you no idea where value is created.

Value curve (arguably David Weinstein among others). This helps you identify what your customers really value about your offering. Ask your customers to rank or rate every aspect of your offering and then draw the results on a graph: it will look like a curve from most important to least important. Then look at where you spend your costs and focus your effort: the chances are that there is a mismatch. You can now cut back on what the customer least values and invest in what the customer wants most. The result: a lower cost, more valued and highly competitive offering.

Value proposition. This answers the question 'what value or benefit will we offer our target customer?' More prosaically: 'why will they give us their money?' This is a vital concept to master and question to answer.

40

Developing strategy in the middle of the organization

The challenge

Most strategy advice, research and work is focused on the top of the firm. In practice, you need to understand and deploy strategy long before you reach the C-suite. It is too late to learn strategy when you are in the corner office, and you probably will not get there anyway if you have not been able to act strategically much earlier in your career.

So what does strategy mean if you are leading a team or a function within the firm?

The solution

Strategy in the middle is about alignment: show that you can align what you are doing with the strategic direction of the firm. If you can do this, you will be noticed and loved by the CEO. The CEO will talk endlessly about the new direction of the firm, and needs managers to take initiative and act on those words. Not all the initiative can come from the top, but that is exactly what many managers expect: they want to be told what to do. It is easier to follow directions than to take the risk of doing something different. As a leader, you have to step up and take initiative. Find a creative way of interpreting the new strategic direction, and apply it to your part of the business. Then you will be living up to the definition of a leader: you will be taking people where they would not have got by themselves.

Strategy in the middle is about alignment

Two examples will make the point of how you can make a difference by showing real alignment with the new strategy from the top.

The risk manager

The new CEO of the bank decided that the goal of the bank would be to become the most customer-focused bank in the market. What on earth has that got to do with risk management? Risk is deep in the bowels of the bank and risk managers can spend their entire career without ever seeing a customer. The CRO (Chief Risk Officer) wanted to remain relevant, so he decided to spend at least one day a month in branches seeing how clients were treated. He discovered that risk and compliance procedures were a huge obstacle to doing business with clients. Some of those obstacles were valid: the bank had to avoid bad risks, bad money and bad clients. But in talking to bank staff, he quickly saw many ways in which risk and compliance procedures could become more customer focused and friendly. Over 18 months, he made risk and compliance the most customer-focused risk and compliance function on the market.

The facilities manager

Facilities management is another role that tends to be deep in the bowels of the organization and is frequently overlooked in strategy discussions. How can you be strategic about cleaning toilets?

The facilities manager heard that the firm wanted to emphasize teamwork and client focus. He realized that was his chance to start a revolution in the professional services firm where he worked, but was usually ignored. His plan was radical:

- Eliminate all private offices, starting with the partners' offices.
- Turn the office into a huge collaboration space with meeting rooms and hot desks: assume most professionals will work at the client site or from home. The only point of being in the office is to meet and collaborate.
- Enable everyone to work from home, with all the right kit and compliance with data protection.
- Create a very fancy client wing, with fancy private dining rooms and a top chef, to woo and impress important clients. This would be funded by the savings from reducing the office space for staff.

There was uproar about his plans and violent opposition from traditionalists. That is the price of leadership. It is hard to take people where they would not have gone by themselves. Eventually, he achieved his revolution and 90 per cent of staff loved it, and 10 per cent left.

Aligning your strategy with that of the firm is not passive management: it can be revolutionary leadership.

41

Developing strategy for the whole organization

The challenge

How can you plan for a future which is inherently unknowable? The world of strategy gives us two different answers.

Design the future through analysis. This is the traditional form of strategy. It is the classical world of action and reaction. Its high priests are Porter and his Five Forces, plus some of the traditional consulting firms with their grids, analysis and impressive PowerPoint presentations. This approach often works best in established firms where you are working in an established market with established competitors, all of which can be analysed at length. The result tends to be incremental change (launch a new product, revamp a service etc.) or a shuffling of the cards (buy and sell various business units).

Discover the future through innovation, trial and error. This is the postmodern form of strategy where you do not plan for an unknowable future: you create the future where you will succeed. Its

Create the future where you will succeed

high priests are the late CK Prahalad and Gary Hamel (strategic intent and core competence), plus some acolytes such as Chan Kim (Blue Ocean Strategy). This approach is best for new entrants and disruptors in existing markets, and for new markets. The ideal result is a completely new way of competing in a market. This is the hallmark of many Silicon Valley start-ups which aim to disrupt existing markets or create new ones.

This chapter explores both options briefly.

The solution

Design the future through analysis

There is an apocryphal story about how consulting firms plan their strategy engagements:

- First third of the time finding the solution
- Second third of the time selling in the solution
- Last third of the time selling the next engagement

The story reveals an essential truth: finding the answer is only a small part of the challenge. The bigger challenge is persuading everyone to accept the solution and then act on it. The challenge is acute for the traditional form of strategy analysis and development. The traditional approach is ideally suited to a black box approach where clever people do stacks of analysis and then come up with a brilliant solution. And then they have a problem persuading mere mortals, who are not as clever as they are, to accept their solution and act on it.

People rarely commit to solutions they do not own. This means that even if you bring in brilliant people to do your strategy work, you need to bring your own team along with you. You have to make sure that your team is meaningfully involved at every stage of the strategy development process: that is more than having a 50-minute interview with the consultants. It will involve workshops, roadshows and town hall meetings during the design process. This is not just about democracy and ownership: it is about finding the best ideas and best solutions. Some of the best insights do not come from analysing market trends: they come from talking to front-line staff, talking to suppliers and customers and watching how people use your product or service.

The process of selling the solution does not start when you have the solution. It starts as soon as you start the strategy process. Involve people early and often.

Discover the future through action

Many of the greatest enterprises today did not start with a long and brilliant analysis of today's markets. They started with someone having a great idea and having the courage to pursue their dream: 25 years ago, social media was unknown, paid search hardly existed and the only electric vehicles were old-fashioned milk floats with a top speed of 10kph. Discovering the future can make you a billionaire.

This approach sounds great, but has three problems:

1. How do you come up with the great idea?
2. How do you manage the risk?
3. How do you bring people with you?

How do you come up with a great idea?

It helps if you are a driven genius (Steve Jobs, possibly) or you get lucky (IBM asked Bill Gates to provide an OS for their new PC business, and the rest is history). Being a lucky genius is best of all. But for the rest of humanity, there are three ways for you to come up with a great idea:

- Copy or adapt an idea. Ryanair carries more passengers in Europe than any other airline and is a straight derivative of the pioneer Southwest Airlines in the United States.
- Solve a problem. James Dyson was annoyed that vacuum cleaners lost power. Over 5,000 prototypes later, he found an answer which changed an industry.
- Fail fast, learn fast – which is often branded as expeditionary marketing and strategy. Keep trying new ideas

Fail fast, learn fast at small scale; learn from each failure and then rapidly scale the successes. You can focus your tests with some simple research: involve customers (existing and potential) and suppliers in your strategy process and do workshops or focus groups with them.

How do you manage the risk?

Radical strategy and expeditionary marketing faces two risks: one risk is that you fail, the other is that you succeed.

You can reduce the risk of failure by taking the fail fast, learn fast approach. Small losses at the outset are manageable and avoid large losses at the end. When you go to scale, you will have a model which you know works.

The risk of success is more problematic. If you find a radical new way of competing, you inevitably attack and cannibalize your own business. Kodak knew that digital photography would kill the film business, but they could not afford to destroy that profitable business, until it was too late for them to win the digital battle. Giving up your profit sanctuary and abandoning a successful business model is very hard to do for both logical reasons (when do you take the profit hit?) and political reasons (many managers inside your firm will rightly fear that they are not part of the brave new future).

How do you bring people with you?

Discovering the future is risky, and people do not like risk. So you have a problem.

If you want incremental change, the risk is manageable. You can encourage your team to do their own version of discover the future: let them learn fast and fail fast with lots of micro-innovations. They will control the process, own it and be committed to it.

The real problem starts if you want radical change. That is a threat to existing managers in their existing roles, and they will find every reason to kill the process and to sabotage your efforts. In practice, larger firms find the best way to deal with the problem is to avoid it. Instead of trying to bring the existing business and its managers with you, create a completely different unit which can think and act like a start-up. These skunk works are insulated from the old business and old ways of thinking and doing things. You do not need to turn the old guard into the new guard. You create an entirely new guard and challenge them to become the new future.

People value the discovered truth more than they believe the dictated truth. If you tell someone the answer they may or may not believe it. If they work the answer out for themselves, they will believe it completely. This means they will be committed to making the solution work. They will identify solutions to problems and overcome problems without always having to delegate problems back up to you. Helping people discover the truth takes more time at the start, but saves much more time when it comes to making it happen.

PART SEVEN

MANAGE YOUR CAREER

42

Learn your unique success formula

The challenge

I ask groups how they have learned to lead. I give them six options and let them pick the two most important sources of learning. See which two sources you would pick:

- Books
- Courses
- Bosses (good and bad lessons)
- Role models (inside or outside work)
- Colleagues/peers
- Experience

Virtually no one chooses books or courses, which could be bad news for an author that runs leadership courses. Nearly everyone chooses some mix of personal experience and observed experience. That makes sense. You discover what works for you in your context and do more of it. You mess up, and resolve not to make that mistake again. Experience lets you create your personal success model.

Experience lets you create your personal success model

The bad news about experience is that it is a random walk to the future. Bump into good projects, experiences and bosses and you accelerate your career. Bump into poor experiences and career becomes a verb: you career into a dead end. Learning from experience is also a good way to keep junior people junior: make them wait their turn. You need a way to accelerate your learning from experience.

The good news about books and courses is that they can help you put some structure on your random walk of experience and they can help you make sense of the nonsense you encounter. They can accelerate your learning and your career. But you cannot do a one-day course, or even read a book, and emerge as a complete leader at the end of it. You need a way of accelerating your learning from experience, which is the focus of the solution below.

The solution

You can accelerate your leadership learning, and that of your team, by making the most of all experiences, good or bad. Here is how.

After any significant event, which might be as simple as a meeting or an important call, take a moment to reflect and learn from it. Do not rush on to the next vital thing on your to-do list. Good learning is like gold dust: capture it, store it and keep it for use in the future. You can do this by asking two simple questions: WWW and EBI.

WWW

WWW asks 'what went well?' This is the essential first question. Many managers learn from bitter and adverse experience, and are often poor at learning from success. Learning from success is how you can build your personal success formula about what works for you in your context: it will be theory free, but practical and relevant. Asking WWW enables you and your team to find out what works well for you. This does not have to be a big formal review. You can ask yourself this question in a minute or two as you walk from one meeting to the next. Make it easy for yourself.

Asking WWW is especially important after a difficult event where things went awry. Even at such moments, you probably did something which meant that you stopped a problem becoming a disaster. That is very valuable knowledge to bottle.

Do not ask WWW's evil twin: 'what went wrong?' That is a recipe for arguments, politicking and negativity in which you will learn nothing. Instead, you can ask a more positive question which will let you learn: EBI.

EBI

EBI asks 'Even better if…'. After you have explored what you did well (WWW) you can explore what you could improve next time (EBI). For instance, when I do this exercise with experienced sales people, they normally identify very simple EBI statements, such as 'it would have been even better if...

- I listened more and talked less
- I had asked more questions
- I had prepared more carefully for the call'

These are more productive statements than:

- 'Why can't you shut up for once?'
- 'Why do you always try making smart points all the time?'
- 'Don't you ever prepare properly for a call?'

WWW and EBI may not reveal some mysterious secret of leadership, but it will help you reinforce basic disciplines consistently, and will help you create your own secret sauce of leadership success.

WWW and EBI is strong both as a personal tool and as a team tool. When your team is in the habit of debriefing constructively, they will learn and improve fast and they will be positive and constructive in their criticism of each other. You will have a positive and high-performing team working for you.

43

Gain promotion

The challenge

Promotion should be a rational process in which the best people levitate up into leadership roles. A quick look around your own organization is likely to challenge that idea. Working hard and working well is rarely enough to get promoted, for three reasons:

1. There are normally too many talented people chasing too few promotions. You may be good, but so are your colleagues. You need to find a way of standing out.
2. Assessment systems rarely identify the best talent. Ninety-five per cent of staff are rated as above average in most assessment systems. This is statistically impossible but emotionally inevitable, because no one believes that they are below average. The more competitive the environment, the more the rating system becomes skewed. In one investment bank staff who scored 9.9/10 were doing well, 9.8 was just about acceptable and 9.7 meant that you were about to be fired.
3. Promotion criteria become increasingly unclear as you become more senior. Expectations are clear for entry-level staff. There are no rules for how you move from being a C-suite executive to becoming CEO. In practice, this means that you have to become increasingly proactive in seeking promotion as your career progresses: you have to make your case, because no one else will make it for you.

The solution

Performing well against targets is your entry ticket into the leadership race. If you are not meeting targets, you are not in the race. If you are meeting them, you give yourself a chance. Once you have your entry ticket, there are five things you need to do:

Working hard and working well is rarely enough to get promoted

1. Work on promotable work

This sounds obvious, but the obvious is often ignored. In any firm, most work is routine: you keep the machine working, but you are not building a new machine. Being asked to organize a leaving party shows you are liked, but is not the road to promotion. But every firm and every team has a few vital projects which will make a difference. These are the assignments you need to work on if you are to be noticed. Do not assume that you will be given promotable work automatically. You have to identify the right projects and then ask to be put on them. Control your destiny.

2. Have a claim to fame

If everyone else is performing well, you need something which makes you stand out from the crowd. You need a claim to fame.

Fortunately, there are always crises and opportunities emerging in any organization. When they first emerge, no one is quite sure what to do, or who should do it and there are no resources for it anyway. That is your moment to step up and deal with the crisis or opportunity. You may have to invest personal discretionary time, but top management

When you step up, you stand out

will be delighted to see someone showing initiative and taking a problem away from them. When you step up, you stand out. You shine in a way that colleagues who stick to the day job cannot shine.

3. Stake your claim

It is not enough to have a claim to fame. You need to stake your claim. You need to be able to tell a story about why you are special. Of course, you know you are special. But unfortunately, bosses two levels up are responsible for perhaps 50 special people, and they have their own crises and opportunities to attend to. Your career will be a lower priority for them than buying the dog food. If they forget the dog food they will have to deal with an unhappy dog and unhappy household. If they forget about your career, there are another 49 people they can fall back on.

You need to create a simple narrative about why you stand out from everyone else. The narrative has to be as short as a newspaper headline, because no one will remember all the details of how you brilliantly beat budget by 3.2 per cent in Q3. The headline is going to be as simple as you are the person who 'brought in major client X' or 'introduced new product Y to the market' or 're-organized business Z'.

4. Ask for promotion

If you don't ask the question, you don't get the answer. It may seem obvious that you have to apply, but many people still think that the opportunity will come to them. Perhaps at a junior level, the opportunity will come your way. As you progress, you have to become more proactive and seek out new roles. This leads to two traps, which are easy to fall into.

The first, obvious, trap is failing to apply for promotion. This often happens because you look at the role description and it is often written so that only Wonder Woman or Super Man qualify. No leader ticks all the boxes, and every promotion candidate is a compromise against the ideal outlined in the job description. You will never meet all the criteria, and you do not need to. You simply need to be less of a compromise than all the other compromised candidates.

The second trap is take feedback seriously, in the event that you do not get the role you wanted. Inevitably, the selection panel has to make up a story

If you don't ask the question, you don't get the answer

about why each unsuccessful candidate was not offered the role. The danger is that you believe their story and then spend two years trying to rectify the shortcomings that the panel claim to have found in you. Once again, this is forcing you to live up to an ideal which no one can achieve. You can waste years trying to do this. Instead of using the feedback to change how you work, use the feedback to change how you interview for your next role: the feedback will be useful in helping you pitch your story even better next time around.

There is gender bias here. Experience from one programme which prepared senior teachers to become head teachers showed that men would apply for headships when they were about 50 per cent ready: they would try to blag their way into the role and then learn on the job. If they were unsuccessful, they assumed the selection panel had made a mistake and they would keep on applying until they got lucky. Females tended to wait until they were at least 90 per cent ready. If rejected, they would take the feedback and spend some years working on their professional development.

5. Be visible

Senior managers are only dimly aware of what more junior staff are really doing. They form their impressions of individuals from a few chance encounters. Make the most of these encounters, which may be planned or unplanned.

Planned encounters give you the chance to shine. This might be a presentation you make, a report you prepare or a meeting you attend. Invest extra time and effort in making sure you do your best, act your best and look your best.

Unplanned encounters are also an opportunity. Surprisingly, you can plan for unplanned encounters. You know that you are likely to meet senior people in the corridor or at the water cooler, or perhaps at the side of a meeting. If you know that you will meet them, but you do not know when, it makes sense to be ready. At minimum, put your best face on: professional, positive and energetic because impressions count. At best, be ready with a question or comment for them. Just asking for their insight and advice on something is a good way to flatter them: it shows that you value their judgement.

44

Manage your career

The challenge

Your career progress and survival depends on your ability to keep on learning. You have to keep on re-inventing yourself. The table below shows how the rules of survival and success change at each level of the organization. Learning is not nice to have, it is a must-have priority.

	Entry level employee	First line manager	Middle manager	Senior manager
Key skills	Technical: audit, research, legal, coding etc.	People skills: managing team	Organization skills: managing politics	Strategic skills: leading change
Key task	Doing things reliably	Making things happen through other people	Managing managers	Managing the organization
Time horizon	Today	Week/month	This quarter	This year and beyond
Amount of freedom and control	Low: do as you are told	Tightly defined discretion	High complexity: competing agendas, inadequate resources	High control but high ambiguity: set the agenda

Financial perspective	Minimum financial responsibility	Control costs	Negotiate and manage budgets	P&L management: cost allocation, revenue generation
Who you rely on	Self	Your team	Other functions and departments	Support staff: finance, HR etc.

The changing rules of survival and success means that each promotion is a moment of great peril. What worked for you in your last role will not work for you in your next role. You have to set aside your old success model and learn a new success model. Few people achieve this, and few people reach top leadership positions. If you can keep on learning and changing, you can be one of the few.

Promotion is a moment of great peril

At its simplest, your career moves from learning technical skills (to become an auditor or teacher, for instance) to learning people and political skills so that you can lead teams and organizations. These are radically different skill sets. Use the table above to see if you are building the skills you need for your future.

The solution

In theory, training is the solution. In practice, firms provide too little training, normally of the wrong sort. Up to 98 per cent of managers believe that more training is required. The training that is available is often focused on technical skills for more junior staff. The more senior you become, the more you need to develop the skills of influence, persuasion, managing politics, dealing with crises and conflict. There is little training that helps with any of this. Instead, you have to ensure you gain the right experiences so that you can learn from experience.

To advance your learning and your career, you need the right experiences at the right time. In theory, you should be able to rely on the goodwill and support of your boss and the HR department to look after your interests. In theory, there should not be war, famine and disease. In reality, both your boss and your HR department will not see your career as their top priority. You have to manage your career yourself.

You should be able to identify the death star projects and managers in your firm. It is hard to escape such career black holes when you enter them, so you have to avoid them. You can do this by making yourself both busy and indispensable in your current role.

You should also be able to identify assignments which will help your career. These assignments will meet the following criteria:

1. Play to your strengths. But if this is all you do, you will never grow and learn new skills.
2. Build new skills that you want for the future. Avoid succeeding at things you do not want to do. Check the skills matrix table to see if you will develop the sorts of skills you will need for your next promotion.
3. Work for a supportive boss who you trust.
4. Be visible to senior management. You need a claim to fame to advance your career.
5. The project must have a realistic chance of success: right resources, budget, goals and support.

To find these assignments, work the grapevine to find out what new ideas and projects are emerging. Senior managers always have new initiatives where they need some help to shape the idea and

Avoid succeeding at things you do not want to do

build momentum. This is your chance to step up and offer to help, using discretionary time and effort. If you help shape the plan, the chances are that you will be asked to help deliver it. You can bypass the formal HR systems completely and take control of your career.

Landing these assignments puts you in competition with your peers. Being the first mover and offering help at the outset puts you in a strong position. Normally, this means you need to be in the office (unless your firm is 100 per cent remote). It is easier to be in the information flow in the office, and easier to nudge decision makers by 'accidentally' bumping into them in the corridor, at the water cooler or over lunch.

Take control of your career. Just as every leader is different, so every career is different. Each of us are on a unique journey of a lifetime. It will have highs and lows, but whatever your journey is, enjoy it.

Index

accountability, embracing 29–31
adversity, resilience in 25–8
agenda relevance, meeting 51, 52
aggressive colleagues 89, 90, 91
Agile project management 147
Alexander the Great 37
alignment, personal 56
alignment, professional 57
ambiguity of professional work 73, 74–5
ambition 9–12, 26, 93
analysis, design the future through 176, 177
applications, job 188–9
appraisals 82
   see also feedback
Art of War (Sun Tzu) 155–6
assertiveness 90–1
assessment systems, performance 186
assumptions and financial analysis 68–70
autonomy, professional 22, 29, 114, 131

BCG Group 171
'bite-sized chunks' of work 148–9
blue ocean strategy 170, 176
bonuses/financial rewards 22–3
boss, managing/leading your 92
   how to adapt to your boss 94–5
   how to mess up with your boss 94
   what your boss wants from you 92–4
boundaries and breaks, working 42–4, 49
Branson, Richard 43–4
bravery/courage 17
   incremental training 18–19, 61

practise 19–20
structure and support 19
breaks and boundaries, work 42–4, 49
budgets/budget management 130, 133, 144–5, 156
Buffett, Warren 43
'burning platforms' 104, 142–3
business reading 66–7

case study interviews 166–9
cash flow 169
catastrophizing 27
CEOs/C-suite execs 36, 104, 132, 143, 144, 145–6, 173, 186
Chan Kim 170
changes, making 4, 141
   N x V x C x F > R change equation 142–6
    C – capability and capacity for change 144–5
    F – first steps 145–6
    N – need for change 142–3
    R – risks and costs of change 146
    V – vision for the change 143–4
Churchill, Winston 2, 3, 157
'claims to fame' 152, 187
closing conversations 59
co-creation 170
coaches 19, 63
coaching your team 77–8, 84, 130
   5 'O' model 78–9
    1. objectives 79
    2. overview 79–80
    3. options 80
    4. obstacles 80–1
    5. outcome 81

commitment process   145–6
competitive advantage   167–8, 171
confidence   153
conflicts, dealing with
         organizational   155–7
constructive dissent   119, 155
control and leadership   137–40
control freak managers   5, 120
copying/adapting ideas   178
core competences   168, 171, 176
courses and literature,
         professional   183, 184
Covid-19 global pandemic   4
credibility   102–3
crises management   97, 153, 158, 187
   style   158–9
   substance/actions   159–62
criteria, clarity of promotion   186
critical paths, identifying project   149
criticism/negative feedback   82, 84,
         118, 119
culls, management   85
customers   166–7, 169, 172

deadline clarity   31
debriefs, learning from   19, 52, 67,
         115, 184–5
decision making   51, 52, 118, 126, 150,
         160–1
decisiveness   97
declining baselines   141
delegation   35, 49, 114, 118, 120,
         128–31, 133
delegation, upward   73, 77
demotivation, avoiding   117, 118–19
difficult people, dealing with   89–91
digital communication technology   5,
         121, 122
dishonesty   94
disloyalty   94
distractions/noise, avoiding   48–9,
         130–1, 133
diversity, team   139–40
doubt and ambiguity   97

dress and behaviour   153–4
Dyson, James   178

early wins   145
EBI 'even better if' discussions   127,
         184–5
ending a presentation   63
energy, managing your   26, 41–4
EQ (Emotional Quotient)   4
excuses   11, 36, 37, 94
expectations, managing   103
experience, learning from   183–5
external stakeholder relations   102
extrinsic rewards   22, 112–13

Facebook   169
facilities management   174–5
fads, management   143
'fail fast, learn fast'   178, 179
family/home life   43–4, 99, 114, 161
fear of public speaking   60, 61
feedback   19, 82, 188
   focus on positive feedback   83, 119
   having adult to adult
         conversations   84
   normalizing feedback   84, 86–7,
         119
financial analysis   68–70, 168–9
financial/extrinsic rewards   22, 112–13
finders   53
Five Forces   171, 176
focus, project/priority   130, 133

Gates, Bill   43, 178
gender biases   188–9
goal alignment   102, 156, 173
goal clarity   22, 30, 48, 75, 86, 118, 148
goal setting   73–6, 172
Google   169
governance systems, project   150
gratitude, showing   36
'Great Resignation' (2021–22) 115
grinders   53
growth/share matrix   171–2

Hamel, Gary   171, 172, 176
Hammer and Champy   172
HBOS business banking   11
high-performance teams, appealing to
        96–9, 107–8
hobbies/interests   43–4
holidays, taking   44
home and hybrid working   4, 47, 48–9,
        50, 102, 115, 120–7
honesty   97–8
hosting meeting   52
HR departments   107, 108, 130, 133

IBM   178
ideas, coming up with great   169, 178
imposter syndrome   31–3
incremental training, courage and
        18–19, 61
inertia, organizational   140, 142
influence, having   36, 151–4
informal power, growing   151, 152
inherited processes and inertia
        140
innovation/action, discover the future
        through   176, 177–9
intelligence   93
interference, managing   130
internal chatter   26–7
interviews   31–2, 188
IPM (idea, people, money and machine)
        agenda   107, 132, 138
    ideas – RUSSIA model   138–9, 140
    money and machine   140
    people   139–40
IQ (Intelligence Quotient)   4

job applications   31–2
job crafting   23–4
Jobs, Steve   37, 178

Kodak   178–9

leadership
    ambition   9–12, 26

appealing to followers   96–9,
        107–8, 153
becoming a leader   3–4
bravery/courage   17–20
building trust   100–4, 153
career management   190–3
coaching   77–81
contextual nature of   3
crises management   158–62
dealing with difficult people   89–91
dealing with poor performance
        85–8
defining   4
delegating well   128–31
financial analysis   68–70
gaining promotions   186–9
giving feedback   82–4
goal setting   73–6
growing your influence   151–4
impossibility of perfection   3, 31,
        96, 100
knowing your role   132–3
leading/building remote teams
        120–7
leading on your own terms   4
leading your boss   92–5
learning leadership   183–5, 190
making change happen   141–6
meeting productivity   50–2
mindset   9–10
motivation   21–4, 97, 110–19
optimism/positivity   13–16, 26–7
organizational conflict/battles
        155–7
persuasive presenting   60–3
persuasive talking   53–9
project management   147–50
reading with purpose   66–7
resilience   25–8
selective unreasonableness   37–40
strategy   165–80
taking control   137–40
taking responsibility   29–32
team coaching   77–81

teams/support   3–4, 31, 34–6
workplace productivity   47–50
writing with impact   64–5
learning and leadership   22, 24, 114,
    115, 116, 127, 183–5, 190–2
learning culture, developing a   115
learning/growth, adversity and   27–8
listening, importance of   36, 54, 57,
    67, 76, 80
loyalty   119

management culls   85
management styles, clash of   85, 86,
    94–5
managers vs leaders   9–10
Maslow's hierarchy of needs   111–12,
    116
Masters of Business Administration
    (MBA)   38
McGregor's Theory of X and Y
    112–13
meeting length   43
meeting performance, learning
    from   51–2
meeting productivity   50–2
meeting protocols   126
memorable phrases, using   63
Methods Adoption Workshops   125–7
MetLife   108–9
minders   53
mission driven organizations   23, 24
monitoring progress   31, 150
motivation   21–4, 97, 110–19, 131
multi-tasking   48
Musk, Elon   37
Myers Briggs Type Indicators (MBTI)   95

N x V x C x F > R formula for
    change   142–6
narrative creation and control,
    having   87–8, 94, 152, 161–2,
    188
new entrants to market   171
Nietzsche, Friedrich   27

objections, dealing with   58–9
obstacles, identifying   30–1
offsite events, team/trust
    building   121–2
open questions, asking   55
optimism   13–16, 26, 108–9, 159
ownership, goal   73–4, 76

paraphrasing, power of   54
partnership principle   55
PASSION conversational structure   55
    1. preparation   56
    2. alignment   56–7
    3. situation   57
    4. size the prize   57–8
    5. idea   58
    6. objections   58–9
    7. next steps   59
perceptions, dealing with unhelpful   32–3
performance management/
    assessments   130, 133
    see also feedback
personality tests   95
persuasion
    persuasive presentations   60–3
    persuasive talking   53–9
pessimism/negativity   13, 118, 159
Pichai, Sundar   44
Plan B, having a   59
politics, organizational   52, 69, 79, 85,
    114, 145, 160, 161
poor performance, dealing with   85–8
Porter, Michael   176
Portfolio Strategy   171–2
positive relationships   22, 26
positivity   13–16, 26–7, 83, 118, 159
PQ (Political Quotient)   4
practise, importance of   19–20, 61
Prahalad, CK   171, 172, 176
praise, giving   83, 84, 119, 162
presentations, persuasive   60–3
PRINCE2   147
proactivity   93
problem solving   10–12, 178

productivity, meeting   50–3
productivity, workplace   47–50, 128
professional training   63
profitability   168–9
project choice and opportunities   187, 192–3
project management   147
promotions, gaining   186–9
proposals, evaluating financial   69, 70
proposals, making financial   69, 70
public speaking   60–3
public vs private commitment 145–6
purpose, importance of   22–4, 115

questions, asking smart   57

Ramaswamy, Venkat   170
RAMP model   22, 113–14
re-engineering   172
reaching out/supportive relationships 34–6, 63, 87, 104
reading with purpose   66–7
recruitment   35, 107–9, 129, 133
references, work   107
reliability   93
remote teams, leading/building 120–7
reporting and decision making 150
resilience, building   25–8
resource availability   30, 114, 144–5
responsibility, taking   29–33
risk management   146, 174, 178–9
risks, identifying   30–1, 149–50
risky situations, dealing with   103–4
RUSSIA ideas   138–9
ruthless streaks   39–40
Ryanair   178

selection panels   31–2, 188
self-assessment, staff   130
self-talk/internal chatter   26–7
selling your ideas see persuasion

short interval scheduling   43, 49
short-term goal focus   43
skills development and mastery   22, 24, 114, 115, 116, 127, 190–1, 192
slides, presentation   62
SMART goals   74–5
social alignment   101–2
sponsors, credibility and politics   30–1, 69, 104, 145, 161
spreadsheets and financial analysis 68
staff see teams, leadership and
staking your claim and visibility   152, 187–8, 189
stepping up   29–30, 31–3, 152–3, 160, 187
STIR Education   11
strategic intent   172, 176
strategy/strategic conversations   165
    channels/reaching your customers   167
    competitive advantage   167–8, 171
    considering customer perspective 166–7
    considering financial perspective 168–9
    considering market perspective 166
    developing mid organizational 173–5
    developing strategy for a whole organization
        design the future through analysis   176, 177
        discover the future through innovation/action   176, 177–9
    organizational core competences   168
    top ten strategy concepts   170–2
stress/burnout   6, 25, 34, 41, 44, 73, 97, 137, 144
style, presenting   62

substance and structure,
    presentation   62–3
substitutes, market   171
success, setting up for   30–1
Sun Tzu   155–7
suppliers   171
supportive relationships   24, 34–6, 63,
    87, 104, 116, 151, 161

Taylor, FW 42
Teach First   11
teams, leadership and   3–4, 31, 34–6,
    144–5
    acknowledging staff career
      aspirations   98–9, 114
    appealing to high-performance
      teams   96–9, 107–8
    coaching for performance   77–81,
      130
    dealing with difficult people   89–91
    dealing with poor
      performance   85–8
    delegation   35, 49, 114, 118, 120,
      128–31
    giving feedback   82–4, 86–7, 99,
      114
    goal setting   73–4, 76
    leading/building remote
      teams   120–7
    Methods Adoption
      Workshops   125–7
    motivation   110–19, 131
    selecting the right team   107–9,
      139–40, 156
    WWW and EBI discussions   127,
      184–5
Tesla   168, 169, 171
three Es of effective presentation   61,
    62

Timpson's   109
tiredness/fatigue   41, 49
toxic bosses   6, 22
training, incremental   18–19, 61
training opportunities   183, 184, 191
    see also learning and leadership; skills
      development and mastery
trust   35, 36, 97, 100–4, 118, 120, 121,
    131, 153, 192

unreasonableness, selective   37–40, 89

value chains   172
value curves   170, 172
value proposition   172
values, recruiting for   108–9, 139
values, reviewing   127
venture capitalists   69
victimhood   89, 90, 91
visibility, personal professional   189,
    192
vision for change   143–4
vision, importance of having   97
visualizing success   27, 28, 61
vital projects, identifying   187, 192–3
VUCA crises   161

WIFM 'what's in it for me?' factor
    57–8, 143–4
win/lose conversations   157
work ethic   93
work life balance   43–4, 99, 114
writing with impact   64–5
WWW 'what went well?' meetings
    127, 184

YTH team meetings   122–4

Zoom calls   13, 107, 122